UNBRIELIEVABLE!

HarperCollins*Publishers*
1 London Bridge Street
London SE1 9GF

www.harpercollins.co.uk

HarperCollins*Publishers*
Macken House, 39/40 Mayor Street Upper,
Dublin 1, D01 C9W8, Ireland

First published by HarperCollins*Publishers* in 2024

1 3 5 7 9 10 8 6 4 2

Written by Jassy Davis
Cover design by Jacqui Caulton
Interior design by e-Digital Design
Cover and interior images © Shutterstock
Project editor: Caitlin Doyle

A catalogue record for this book is available from the British Library.
Library of Congress Cataloging-in-Publication Data has been applied for.

ISBN 978-0-00-871129-0

Printed and bound in Latvia

This book is produced from independently certified FSC™ paper
to ensure responsible forest management.

For more information visit: www.harpercollins.co.uk/green

DISCLAIMER:
The publisher urges the reader to drink, eat, and prepare food responsibly. Be advised:
some recipes include nuts or other allergens. Check local food regulations—in particular,
regarding guidance on pastueurized and unpasteurized cheeses in your local area.
Guidance for vegetarians and vegans—some cheese contains rennet, an animal byproduct.
Be sure to check all labeling to ensure your specific brand of cheese is vegetarian or vegan,
as some cheese types (such as feta) can come with or without rennet.

UNBRIELIEVABLE!

FROM CHEDDAR TO STILTON, OVER SIXTY DELECTABLY CHEESY RECIPES FOR BOARDS, BAKES & MORE

JASSY DAVIS

CONTENTS

INTRODUCTION

WELCOME

Cheese has been on the menu for almost 10,000 years. And today, there are at least 2,000 different types of cheese being eaten around the world. There's a cheese for every palate and occasion. From soft, fresh curds eaten on the day they're made, to mature cheeses ripened for months in underground caves and marbled with blue veins. Whether you like your cheese light and lemony, salty and tangy, or rich and stinky, there's a cheese for you. And there's a cheese dish, too. Take your pick from these 60 versatile recipes that will help you make a meal out of cheese at breakfast, lunch, and dinner.

KNOW YOUR CHEESES

There are a lot of different types of cheese to choose from. Knowing the difference between the basic types of cheese will help you work out which ones you like most, and which ones will suit the meals you want to make.

HARD CHEESES
Parmesan, Grana Padano, Manchego, Aged Cheddar

Firm and dense with a crumbly texture and crunch, these full-flavored cheeses pack a punch. They're normally pungent, savory, and rich. Store them wrapped in wax paper in a container in the refrigerator. Perfect for grating over pasta, salads, or soups. They're an essential part of any cheeseboard.

SEMI-HARD CHEESES
Gruyère, Emmental, Monterey Jack, Gouda, Edam

Firm, but not as dry and crumbly as aged hard cheeses,
semi-hard cheeses have an elastic texture and are often earthy,
nutty, and sweet-tasting. Store them in wax paper in a container in the refrigerator.
Enjoy them as part of a cheeseboard, in sandwiches, or melted in dishes like fondue.

SOFT AND FRESH CHEESES
Mozzarella, Ricotta, Burrata, Goat cheese, Feta, Mascarpone, Cottage cheese

Unaged, unripened, and rindless, these cheeses can be
creamy or crumbly and they have a mild flavor. Store
them in the refrigerator and eat within a few days of
opening the package.

They're great raw or cooked, especially in salads
and sandwiches, and used in baking.

SOFT-RIPENED CHEESES
Brie, Camembert, Triple Crème, Humboldt Fog

Creamy cheeses that develop a soft, edible rind as they age.
They're best kept wrapped in wax paper in the fridge.
They can be chalky when they're cold, so let them
sit at room temperature for 30 minutes to 1
hour to soften before serving. Great as part of a
cheeseboard, or use in baked dishes and quiches.

SEMI-SOFT CHEESES

Havarti, Munster, Taleggio, Morbier

These cheeses are lightly pressed in their molds to squeeze out some of the liquid, giving them a soft, supple texture. They range in flavor from buttery to tangy. Wrap them in wax paper, then pop in a container in the refrigerator. These are great melting cheeses for dishes like macaroni cheese, or for adding to grilled sandwiches or topping burgers.

BLUE CHEESES

Gorgonzola, Stilton, Danish Blue, Maytag, Roquefort

The most complex type of cheese out there. Blues often combine the creamy, crumbly texture of the soft cheeses with the pungent flavor of hard cheeses. They have veins of mold running through them, giving the cheeses their distinctive sharp and peppery flavor. Wrap them in wax paper and store in the refrigerator. They're best enjoyed at room temperature, so let them sit out of the refrigerator for 30 minutes to 1 hour before serving. Enjoy them as part of a cheeseboard, or use them in sauces to go with steak and burgers. Please note that in the U.S., Roquefort is banned by the FDA because of the presence of a harmless variation of E. coli.

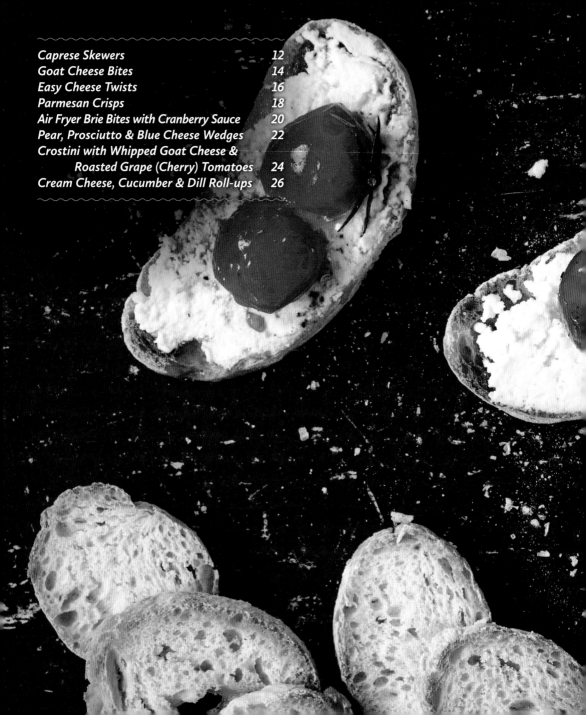

STARTERS & CANAPÉS

CAPRESE SKEWERS

PREP: 20 MINUTES • COOK: NIL • MAKES 8 • VEGETARIAN

When it comes to canapés, I like to keep things simple—not too many ingredients; nothing too time-consuming to make; and with light, fresh flavors that get everyone's tastebuds going. These simple skewers fit the bill perfectly. They're inspired by Italy's most famous salad, which teams creamy mozzarella with juicy, sweet tomatoes and pungent basil leaves. It's a timeless combination that always reminds me of the summer. Bright and bold, with a hint of green, they're the ideal appetizer for get-togethers on sunny days.

12 mini mozzarella balls
24 large fresh basil leaves
16 grape (cherry)
   tomatoes
2 tbsp olive oil
1 tbsp balsamic vinegar
Sea salt and black
   pepper, to taste

Grab 8 wooden skewers. Halve 4 mini mozzarella balls and thread each half onto a skewer. Now thread a large basil leaf onto each skewer. Follow that with a tomato, then another basil leaf, then a mini mozzarella ball. Thread one more basil leaf onto each skewer, then finish with a tomato.

Arrange the skewers on a serving platter. These can be stored in the refrigerator for a couple of hours.

When you're ready to serve the skewers, whisk together the olive oil and balsamic vinegar with a pinch of salt and pepper. Drizzle over the skewers and serve.

If you'd like to turn these into charcuterie skewers, thread a folded half-slice of prosciutto or a round of salami onto the skewers alongside the mozzarella and tomatoes.

GOAT CHEESE BITES

PREP: 15 MINUTES + CHILLING • COOK: NIL • MAKES 12 • VEGETARIAN

If you like your parties to have a vintage vibe, you will love these dinky little Goat Cheese Bites. Little spheres of goat cheese rolled in your pick of coatings, they're a retro choice of canapé that would look brilliant on a buffet table alongside deviled eggs, little sandwiches, and shrimp (prawn) cocktail. They're also a lot of fun to make. Rolling them into balls feels like clay modeling, but instead of clay, you're using cheese. It's important to use the right sort of goat cheese; it needs to be semi-firm with a thin, bloomy rind and a supple texture. This will handle being shaped without melting in your hands. I tend to leave the rind on, even though it makes it difficult to roll perfectly spherical balls. For a neater effect, slice the rind off the cheese with a small, sharp knife before you start rolling.

4oz (120g) semi-firm goat cheese log

Crackers or oat cakes, to serve (optional)

COATINGS:

4 tbsp finely chopped fresh chives, flat leaf parsley, or tarragon

1 tbsp crushed pink or black peppercorns

1 tbsp smoked paprika or sumac

1 tbsp each poppy seeds and sesame seeds, mixed together

Slice the goat cheese into 12 rounds. Roll each round into a ball with the palms of your hands. Make them as round as you can. Place on a plate and set aside.

Pick your coating. You can use one coating or have a mixture to add color and variety. Sprinkle your choice of coatings onto different plates. Roll the balls of cheese in the coatings until evenly coated. Pop them back on the plate and refrigerate for at least 30 minutes to firm up. You can make the bites the day before you want to serve them.

Take the Goat Cheese Bites out of the refrigerator 15–30 minutes before you want to serve them. Serve by themselves with cocktail sticks, or with crackers or oat cakes.

EASY CHEESE TWISTS

PREP: 30 MINUTES • COOK: 12–15 MINUTES • MAKES 16–30 • VEGETARIAN

The ultimate lazy canapé, all you need to make Cheese Twists is a sheet of ready-made puff pastry and some cheese. The trickiest bit is deciding what cheese to use. I like a good, strong Cheddar because it's a great all-rounder—lots of tangy flavor and it melts beautifully. If you'd prefer something milder, you could use Colby or a young Dutch Gouda. For Cheese Twists with a nutty, fruity flavor, use French Comté or Cantal. These twists are best eaten warm from the oven. For parties, assemble the twists and keep them in the refrigerator. Bake them in the oven 30 minutes before your guests arrive, then let them cool for 10 minutes before bringing them out with a round of drinks.

4oz (125g) mature
   Cheddar cheese
All-purpose (plain) flour,
   for dusting
11oz (320g) ready-rolled
   puff pastry sheet
1 medium egg, to glaze
Sesame seeds, to garnish

Preheat the oven to 400°F/200°C/Fan 180°C/Gas 6. Line a baking sheet with parchment (baking) paper. Coarsely grate the Cheddar.

Dust your work surface with a little flour and unroll the puff pastry sheet onto it. Sprinkle the grated Cheddar evenly over the pastry. Take one of the short edges of the pastry and fold it over to the middle of the sheet. Then take the other short edge and fold it over the top of that, so you have a small rectangle. Roll the cheese-filled pastry back out to make a ¼in (½cm) thick rectangle. You can slice the rectangle in half widthways to make short twists or leave it large to make longer twists.

Slice the pastry into strips approximately ½in (1cm) thick. Carefully lift each strip and twist it a few times to give it a spiral shape. Place the twists on the baking tray, leaving a little gap between each twist.

Crack the egg into a bowl and beat it with 1 tablespoon of water. Brush the twists with egg to glaze. Sprinkle over a few pinches of sesame seeds.

Bake for 12–15 minutes or until the twists are puffed up and golden brown. Remove from the oven and let them cool for a few minutes on the baking tray before transferring to a wire rack. Serve warm or cold. They will keep in an airtight container for up to 3 days.

PARMESAN CRISPS

PREP: 5 MINUTES • COOK: 12–15 MINUTES • MAKES 20

These crunchy snacks are one of the best things to come out of the low-carb trend. Crisp wafers of pure cheese, they make a satisfying pre-dinner bite. Pile them into bowls for parties, serve them as part of a grazing board, or use them as a garnish for pasta and risotto dishes. Parmesan isn't vegetarian because it's made with calf rennet, so if you want to make a veggie-friendly version, look out for vegetarian "Parmesan-style" hard cheeses and use one of those instead. You can also make these crackers with Grana Padano or Pecorino Romano, which can be a bit more cost-effective. Although they're delicious just made from Parmesan, you can spice things up by mixing in seasonings such as garlic granules, black pepper, dried mixed Italian herbs, or mixed seeds, before baking. Tailor the flavors to suit your tastes.

3½oz (100g) Parmesan cheese

Preheat the oven to 375°F/190°C/Fan 170°C/Gas 5. Line a large baking sheet with parchment (baking) paper.

Finely grate the Parmesan. Scoop up 1 heaped teaspoon of Parmesan and drop it onto the baking sheet. Repeat until you've used up all the cheese. Make sure you leave a gap around each mound so the cheese can spread as it melts.

Bake for 12–15 minutes or until the Parmesan Crisps are golden brown and crisp-looking at the edges.

Remove from the oven and let them cool for 1 minute. Then lift off the sheet with a spatula. Transfer to a wire rack to cool completely. They're ready to eat when they're firm and crisp. The Parmesan Crisps will keep in an airtight container at room temperature for up to 7 days.

AIR FRYER BRIE BITES WITH CRANBERRY SAUCE

PREP: 10 MINUTES + FREEZING • COOK: 8–10 MINUTES • SERVES 2 • VEGETARIAN

A crispy, golden-brown breadcrumb shell filled with gooey, melting Brie is hard to resist. This French bistro treat used to be tricky to make at home because it had to be deep-fat-fried. Which can be messy and—no matter how delicious it tastes—the lingering smell of fried cheese is hard to get rid of. But now air fryers are here, and fried Brie is easy and less stinky to make at home. The key to successfully air-frying Brie is to double coat it in breadcrumbs before cooking; this ensures the cheese is sealed inside the panko coating and won't leak. Check your Brie after 8 minutes: it should be cooked through by then, and if there is a little gap and the cheese has started to leak out, you can whip it out of the fryer and serve it before any more cheese escapes.

7oz (200g) petit Brie, chilled

2 medium eggs

4oz (120g) panko breadcrumbs

2 heaped tbsp all-purpose (plain) flour

Sea salt and black pepper, to taste

Cranberry sauce, to serve

Take the chilled round of Brie out of the refrigerator and unwrap it. Dip your knife in warm water, then slice it in half horizontally to make 2 rounds. Then slice these in half, so you have four half-moons.

Crack the eggs into a shallow dish and beat together. Sprinkle the breadcrumbs onto another plate. Tip the flour onto a third plate and season with salt and pepper, stirring well to mix.

Dip a piece of Brie into the flour, turning to make sure it's completely coated, then shake off any excess. Dip it into the beaten egg, then dip it into the breadcrumbs. Repeat with all four rounds. Then dip them all into the egg and then the breadcrumbs again. Double-coating the Brie helps stop it leaking when it bakes. Place the coated Brie on a baking sheet and freeze for 1 hour or overnight.

When you're ready to cook the Brie, line your air fryer baskets. Preheat the air fryer to 375°F/190°C. Pop the Brie into the baskets and air-fry for 8–10 minutes or until golden brown and crisp.

Serve the Brie Bites straight away with cranberry sauce.

If you want to bake your Brie in the oven, set it to 375°F/190°C/Fan 170°C/Gas 5. Place the frozen Brie rounds on a baking sheet lined with parchment (baking) paper. Bake for 8–12 minutes, or until golden brown. Serve hot from the oven.

PEAR, PROSCIUTTO & BLUE CHEESE WEDGES

PREP: 10 MINUTES • COOK: NIL • SERVES 2

An autumnal version of the classic Italian appetizer of melon and Parma ham, this simple salad is made with the mouthwatering combination of juicy pears and fiery blue cheese. I like using Roquefort— France's most famous blue cheese. It's salty and tangy with veins of peppery blue mold running through the paste. If you live in the U.S. and can't get your hands on Roquefort, use Stilton or Danish Blue in its place. The cheese is a delicious foil for the pear's sweetness. Add a few slices of prosciutto di Parma and a handful of arugula (rocket) and you have an elegant starter.

2oz (50g) Roquefort, Stilton, or Danish Blue
4 slices of prosciutto di Parma
2 ripe pears
1 tbsp honey
A handful of arugula (rocket) leaves
Black pepper, to taste

About 30 minutes before you want to assemble these wedges, take the blue cheese and prosciutto out of the fridge and let them warm up a little. This helps the flavors bloom.

Quarter the pears and slice out the cores. Pop them on a serving plate.

Crumble the blue cheese over the pear wedges. Halve the slices of prosciutto and drape a half over each pear wedge. Drizzle over a little honey and grind over some black pepper.

Scatter a handful of arugula (rocket) leaves over the pear wedges and serve.

CROSTINI WITH WHIPPED GOAT CHEESE & ROASTED TOMATOES

PREP: 15 MINUTES • COOK: 35 MINUTES • SERVES 4–6 • VEGETARIAN

Silky whipped goat cheese is quickly going to become your go-to ingredient for entertaining. It's incredibly versatile, you can serve it as a dip, use it to fill filo parcels, or spread it on toasted bread to make crostinis, like these. Whipping the goat cheese with lemon and honey lightens the cheese and softens the flavors. A soft, fluffy goat cheese that hasn't been aged is perfect for this recipe. You can add extra flavorings, like chopped soft herbs, toasted spices, or a pinch of grated Parmesan. I've paired the whipped goat cheese simply with roasted tomatoes, but it also goes really well with prosciutto di Parma, salami, sliced figs, or roasted grapes.

1lb (450g) grape (cherry) tomatoes
Olive oil, to drizzle
7oz (200g) soft goat cheese
2oz (50g) Greek yogurt
Zest and juice of 1 lemon
1 tbsp honey
10oz (300g) sourdough bread
Sea salt and black pepper, to taste
Fresh thyme leaves, to garnish

Preheat the oven to 350°F/180°C/Fan 160°C/Gas 4. Place the tomatoes on a baking sheet lined with parchment (baking) paper. Drizzle over a little olive oil and season with salt and pepper. Roast for 15–20 minutes or until they start to burst. Remove from the oven and set aside.

Place the goat cheese, Greek yogurt, lemon zest, and honey in a food processor. Season with black pepper. Whizz until smooth and creamy. Taste and add salt, pepper, more honey, or a squeeze of lemon juice, if you think it needs it. Chill in the refrigerator until needed.

Slice the bread into ½in (1cm)-thick slices. Place on a clean baking sheet and drizzle with olive oil. Bake for 15 minutes or until golden brown. Take the bread out of the oven and let it cool for a few minutes before assembling the crostini.

When you're ready, top each slice of toast with the whipped goat cheese and a few roasted tomatoes. Sprinkle over a pinch of fresh thyme leaves and serve.

CREAM CHEESE, CUCUMBER & DILL ROLL-UPS

PREP: 30 MINUTES • COOK: NIL • MAKES 30 • VEGETARIAN

These dainty, bite-sized appetizers are perfect for summer entertaining. They're light and refreshing with an indulgent, creamy middle. Use full-fat soft cheese for the filling to maximize the contrast between the rich, velvety cheese and the crisp brightness of the cucumber. Cream cheese can be salty, so just season the filling with black pepper to start with, then taste it and add a pinch of salt if you think it needs it. To make these roll-ups more substantial, line the cucumber ribbons with thinly sliced smoked salmon before you top with the cream cheese and roll up.

7oz (200g) full-fat cream cheese
1 lemon
4–5 sprigs of fresh dill
1 cucumber, approximately 14oz (400g)
Salt and black pepper, to taste

Scoop the cream cheese into a bowl. Finely grate in the zest from the lemon and crack in some black pepper. Beat well to mix. Taste and adjust the seasoning.

Pick the dill off the stalks. Discard the stalks. Use a vegetable peeler to peel ribbons off the cucumber, peeling down to the seeded core. You should get around 30 ribbons.

Place one cucumber ribbon on your work surface. Place 1 teaspoon of the cream cheese mixture at one end and top with a dill sprig. Roll up to make a tight cylinder. Transfer to a serving plate. Repeat with the remaining cucumber ribbons, cream cheese, and dill. The roll-ups are best eaten within 2–3 hours of being made.

BOARDS & SHARERS

LOADED CHEDDAR & BACON POTATO SKINS

PREP: 20 MINUTES + COOLING • COOK: 55–75 MINUTES • SERVES 4

Popcorn and nachos are the kings of movie-night snacks, but I think loaded potato skins should have a spot at the table, too. They're an indulgent finger food that you can easily eat in the dark, although I can't promise that when the lights come back on you won't have sour cream all over your t-shirt! When you're making these loaded skins, use palm-sized potatoes that are big enough to eat in two bites. You can prepare the skins ahead, filling them with the cheese and bacon, then store them in the refrigerator until you're ready to bake and serve them.

2¼lb (1kg) potatoes
Olive oil, to drizzle
6 rashers of streaky bacon
5oz (150g) mature Cheddar cheese
A few pinches of smoked paprika
A few pinches of ground cumin
Sea salt, to taste
3½fl oz (100ml) sour cream, to serve
Finely chopped fresh chives, to serve

Preheat the oven to 400°F/200°C/Fan 180°C/Gas 6. Scrub the potatoes, then pat dry with paper towels (kitchen paper). Prick the potatoes with a fork. Rub with olive oil and season with salt.

Place the potatoes directly on the shelf in the oven. Bake for 45–60 minutes or until they're cooked through. Set aside to cool for 10 minutes.

While the potatoes bake, fry the bacon until it's browned and starting to crisp. Drain the bacon on paper towels, then roughly chop. Coarsely grate the Cheddar.

When the potatoes are cool enough to handle, halve them and scoop out most of the flesh, leaving a ¼in (½cm)-thick layer of potato attached to the skin. Place the skins on a baking sheet. The leftover potato can be saved to make hashes or potato cakes.

Dust a little smoked paprika and ground cumin into each potato skin. Sprinkle in the grated Cheddar, then top with the chopped bacon. Bake for 10–15 minutes or until the cheese is melted and golden.

Remove the potato skins from the oven and place on a serving platter. Top with sour cream and chives. Serve straight away.

PROVOLETA

PREP: 15 MINUTES • COOK: 10 MINUTES • SERVES 4

Fans of fried cheese will love this Argentinian dish. It was invented in the mid-twentieth century when Italian immigrant Natalio Alba realized that Argentinians would enjoy a cheese that went well with barbecued meats. He experimented with Provolone until he came up with a cheese that could be barbecued over hot coals. Provoleta is often eaten first as part of an asado (an Argentinian barbecue) before the grilled meats. Outside of Argentina you can make this dish with Italian Provolone—cooking smaller slices of Provolone will work just as well. You can also cook it in a cast-iron pan in the oven, which is perfect if good weather for an outside grill can't be guaranteed.

2 tsp dried oregano
1 tsp dried chili flakes
¾in (1½cm)-thick slice
  of Provolone cheese,
  approximately 14oz
  (400g)
Olive oil, for frying
Crusty bread, to serve

FOR THE CHIMICHURRI:
1oz (30g) fresh flat leaf
  parsley leaves
3 garlic cloves
1 tsp dried chili flakes
3 tbsp red wine vinegar
4fl oz (120ml) extra
  virgin olive oil
Sea salt, to taste

Start by making the chimichurri. Finely chop the parsley. Peel and crush the garlic. Pop them in a bowl with the chili flakes, red wine vinegar, and olive oil. Season with a pinch of salt. Stir well to mix. Set aside.

Preheat the oven to 400°F/200°C/Fan 180°C/Gas 6. Mix the dried oregano and chili flakes together, then sprinkle evenly over the slice of Provolone. Make sure you coat both sides.

Heat a large, oven-proof, cast-iron frying pan over a medium–high heat. Drizzle in a little oil. Add the Provolone and fry for 1–2 minutes, or until golden brown underneath. Carefully flip over and fry for another 1 minute. Transfer the pan to the oven and bake for 6–8 minutes or until the cheese is melted and gooey.

Remove the Provoleta from the oven. Drizzle over a few spoonfuls of the chimichurri. Serve straight away with crusty bread and the rest of the chimichurri.

POUTINE

PREP: 15 MINUTES • COOK: 50–60 MINUTES • SERVES 4

Canada's national dish is a tasty mix of hot fries topped with fresh cheese curds and gravy. Messy and delicious, it was invented accidentally in Quebec in the 1950s. A customer in a rush asked a restaurateur to put his fries and curds in the same paper bag to go. The restaurant owner replied that it would make a *poutine*—Quebecois slang for a mess. A few years later another chef added gravy and a modern classic was born. Cheese curds are essentially unpressed Cheddar cheese. They're produced in the first step of the Cheddar-making process. If they're pressed in a mold and aged, they turn into Cheddar, but left fresh they're a squeaky, mild-flavored cheese. If you can't find cheese curds in your local store, swap in grated mild Cheddar, mozzarella, or halloumi.

2¼lb (1kg) floury potatoes
Sunflower or rapeseed oil, for frying
2 tbsp unsalted butter
2 tbsp all-purpose (plain) flour
10fl oz (300ml) hot beef stock
10fl oz (300ml) hot chicken stock
10oz (300g) cheese curds, room temperature
Sea salt and black pepper, to taste

Peel the potatoes and slice them into French fries, around ½in (1cm) thick. Rinse under cold water to remove as much excess starch as you can, then pat dry with paper towels (kitchen paper).

Heat the oil in a deep-fat fryer to 270°F/130°C. Put the fries into a fryer basket and sink them into the fat. Fry for 8 minutes or until the fries look like they're forming a skin (if your fryer is small, cook them in batches to avoid crowding). Lift out, drain on paper towels, then spread out on a board or baking sheet. Let them cool completely. This can be done the day before you want to make the Poutine. Store in a tub in your refrigerator.

Make the gravy. Melt the butter in a medium-sized pan over a medium heat. Add the flour and stir constantly with a wooden spoon until it forms a smooth paste (this is the roux). Cook and stir for 2 minutes.

Add a splash of hot beef stock to the pan. Cook, stirring, until it's smoothly combined with the roux. Repeat, until you've added all the beef stock, then pour in the chicken stock. Simmer for 5–7 minutes, stirring occasionally, until the gravy has thickened. Taste and add salt and pepper, if needed. Set aside, lid on, to keep warm.

Heat the oil in your fryer back up to 350°F/180°C. Put the fries back in the fryer basket and fry for around 5 minutes or until they're golden brown. Drain on paper towels, tip into a bowl, and toss with a pinch of salt. Cook the fries in batches, if necessary, and keep them warm in a heatproof dish in your oven set to its lowest temperature.

Divide the hot fries between four serving bowls, or one large bowl. Top with the cheese curds. Ladle over the hot gravy. Serve straight away.

MELT-IN-THE-MIDDLE BAKED BRIE

PREP: 5 MINUTES • COOK: 20–25 MINUTES • SERVES 4 • VEGETARIAN

Baked Brie is one of my favorite ways to feed friends. It's so easy. The Brie takes just 5 minutes to prepare and then the oven does all the work. If your Brie comes in a wooden box, you can unwrap it and bake it in that. If not, place it in a small ovenproof dish. Then score it and tuck in the aromatics before baking. When it comes out of the oven, serve it straight away with a spoon so you can dig in and spread it over slices of crusty bread. This recipe also works brilliantly with small rounds of Camembert.

7oz (200g) petit Brie
1 garlic clove
1–2 sprigs of rosemary
1 tbsp runny honey
Black pepper, to taste
Crusty bread, to serve

Preheat the oven to 400°F/200°C/Fan 180°C/Gas 4. Unwrap the Brie and place it in a snug baking dish. Use a small, sharp knife to score a criss-cross pattern into the top of the Brie. Don't cut too deeply—¼in (½cm) will be fine.

Peel and finely slice the garlic. Pull the rosemary leaves off the woody sprigs. Tuck the slivers of garlic and the rosemary into the cuts you made in the Brie. Grind over a little black pepper. Bake for 20–25 minutes or until the Brie is lightly browned and liquid in the middle.

When the Brie is ready, remove from the oven. Drizzle over a little runny honey. Serve straight away with crusty bread.

QUESO DIP

PREP: 20 MINUTES • COOK: 20 MINUTES • SERVES 6 • VEGETARIAN

A good warm cheese dip is the stuff happy parties are made of. Queso Dip is a staple of Tex-Mex cuisine and is served in Mexican restaurants across America. It's a gooey combination of melted cheese and evaporated milk that's flavored with fresh tomatoes and onions along with a pinch of spice. I've added a spoonful of preserved serrano chilies to this version, which makes it extra spicy, but you can leave it out and just rely on the chili powder for heat. I've also used a mix of Cheddar and Asadero cheeses. Asadero is a Mexican cheese with a mild flavor that melts well. You can swap in Oaxaca cheese or use white American cheese or Cheshire cheese instead.

7oz (200g) mature
  Cheddar cheese
7oz (200g) Asadero cheese
1 small onion
2 garlic cloves
7oz (200g) tomatoes
1 tbsp roasted serrano
  chilies (optional)
2 tbsp butter
1 tsp chili powder
1 tsp ground cumin
7fl oz (200ml)
  evaporated milk
Sea salt and black
  pepper, to taste
A handful of fresh cilantro
  (coriander) leaves
Tortilla chips, to serve

Coarsely grate the cheeses. Peel and dice the onion. Peel and crush the garlic. Quarter the tomatoes, scoop out the seeds, then dice. Set a quarter of the chopped tomatoes aside for later. Drain and finely chop the roasted serrano chilies, if you're using them.

Melt the butter in a large pan over a medium heat. Add the chopped onion and fry, stirring often, for 8–10 minutes or until softened but not browned. If it starts to brown, turn the heat down and add a splash of water.

Add the garlic, tomatoes, and serrano chilies. Cook, stirring often, for 6–8 minutes, or until the tomatoes begin to soften. Add the chili powder and cumin. Cook, stirring, for 1 minute. Pour in the evaporated milk and warm until it's just steaming hot.

Reduce the heat under the pan to low. Gradually add the grated cheese, stirring constantly until the cheese is melted and smooth. Season with salt and pepper.

Pour the Queso Dip into a serving bowl. Top with the reserved diced tomatoes. Garnish with torn cilantro (coriander) leaves. Serve with tortilla chips for dipping.

CLASSIC SWISS FONDUE

PREP: 10 MINUTES • COOK: 10–15 MINUTES • SERVES 4-6

Fondue gets its name from the French word *fondre*, which means "to melt." It's a delicious melange of cheese gently melted in dry white wine to make a very moreish dip for bread and boiled potatoes. Fondue sets quite quickly when it starts to cool. If you have a traditional fondue set you can make the fondue in the pot, then place it over the burner at the table to keep it liquid. Otherwise, be ready to eat quickly or to take the dish of fondue back to the kitchen to be reheated on the hob or in the microwave until it's liquid again.

14oz (400g) Gruyère

14oz (400g) Emmental

8fl oz (250ml) dry white wine

2 tbsp lemon juice

1½ tbsp all-purpose (plain) flour

1 garlic clove

Cubed crusty bread, boiled new potatoes, and cornichons, to serve

Coarsely grate the two cheeses and set aside.

Pour the wine and lemon juice into a large pan. Add the flour. Peel and crush the garlic, then add to the pan. Whisk everything together until smoothly combined, then place the pan over a medium heat and bring to a simmer. When the wine is just simmering, reduce the heat to low. It's important not to overheat the pan as this can break the cheese, making your fondue lumpy and oily.

Add a handful of cheese and whisk it into the wine. When it has melted, add the next handful. Repeat until all the cheese has been added and it has melted to form a thick sauce.

Pour the fondue into a serving dish and serve immediately with cubes of crusty bread and boiled new potatoes for dunking, with cornichons to eat on the side.

HOT SHRIMP, SPINACH & CHEESE DIP

PREP: 20 MINUTES • COOK: 40 MINUTES • SERVES 4

A hot shrimp (prawn) dip is a retro classic. This version is made with a mix of mozzarella, Parmesan, and cream cheese, which make a delicious sauce for fried shrimp and baby leaf spinach. I've kept the flavors simple in this dish so you can enjoy its richness, but you could add in a few pinches of Old Bay seasoning, Cajun seasoning, or mixed dried Italian herbs, depending on what your favorite flavors are. Serve this dip straight from the oven when it's hot and bubbling, with plenty of baguette on the side to scoop it all up.

10oz (300g) shelled raw shrimp (prawns)

7oz (200g) baby leaf spinach

3 garlic cloves

1 red chili

Olive oil, to cook

2½fl oz (60ml) vermouth bianco

3½oz (100g) mozzarella

2oz (50g) Parmesan

7oz (200g) full-fat cream cheese

3½fl oz (100ml) heavy (double) cream

Sea salt and black pepper, to taste

Sliced baguette, to serve

Preheat the oven to 350°F/180°C/Fan 160°C/Gas 4. De-vein and roughly chop the shrimp (prawns). Rinse the spinach and shake dry. Peel and crush the garlic. Finely chop the chili, scooping out the seeds and white pith if you prefer less heat.

Warm a splash of olive oil in an ovenproof frying pan over a medium heat. Add the garlic and chili to the pan and fry for 1 minute or until fragrant. Stir in the shrimp. Pour in the vermouth and let it simmer for 2–3 minutes or until it has reduced by half. Add the spinach and cook, stirring, for 4–5 minutes or until wilted and any excess water has bubbled off. Take off the heat.

Drain and coarsely grate the mozzarella. Finely grate the Parmesan. In a mixing bowl, beat together the cream cheese, mozzarella, Parmesan, and cream. Season with salt and pepper.

Add the cheese mix to the shrimps and spinach. Stir until everything is evenly coated. Bake for 25–30 minutes or until the dip is hot, bubbly, and golden brown. Serve straight away with sliced baguette for scooping.

EASY CHEESE GRAZING BOARD

PREP: 15 MINUTES • COOK: NIL • SERVES 8

Whether it's a light meal to share with friends or the savory course to end a dinner party, a cheeseboard is always a good idea. Easy to put together, you just need to pick a couple of complementary cheeses and then add some condiments, crackers, and fresh fruit to cut through the richness. When you're choosing a mix of cheeses, make sure you include at least one soft or semi-soft cheese, a hard cheese that's been aged, and a goat cheese or a blue cheese to add a funkier flavor to your board. A good, crowd-pleasing mix would be a Brie, a Cheddar, and a Stilton. For a simple board, that's all you need. For larger grazing board, like this one, you can start adding in a few extra cheeses and really turn it into a feast.

7oz (200g) petit Camembert
7oz (200g) mature Cheddar cheese
7oz (200g) Limburger
7oz (200g) Stilton
7oz (200g) Emmental
7oz (200 g) wedge Brie
A bunch of grapes
4–8 figs
Mixed crackers
A handful of walnuts
7oz (200g) jar fruit chutney
Basil leaves, to garnish

Take the cheeses out of the fridge 30 minutes before you want to serve them.

When you're ready to assemble the board, place the mini Camembert on the board. Place a bunch of grapes and some figs on the board. Slice or cube the Cheddar and Limburger. Arrange them and the other cheeses on the board. Add grapes and figs to start to fill in the gaps. Tuck in some crackers—allow 6–8 crackers per person.

Serve the cheeseboard with some walnuts and a jar of spiced fruit chutney. Garnish with basil leaves to add a splash of color.

FRESH & LIGHT CHEESE BOARD

PREP: 30 MINUTES • COOK: NIL • SERVES 6

When you put together a cheese-based grazing board it can be tempting to go all in on rich, indulgent flavors. But pairing cheeses with plenty of fresh ingredients will create a cheeseboard that won't leave you in lactose coma. I've used cheeses that run the full range of flavors in this board. Mozzarella is fresh and light, Gouda has a mild, nutty flavor and semi-soft texture, while Gorgonzola Piccante is a punchy blue cheese that's spicy and peppery. Serving them with toasted bread and a mix of ripe avocado, fresh fruit, almonds, olives, and honey means you and your friends can assemble your own DIY bruschetta at the table.

9oz (250g) mozzarella
7oz (200g) Gouda
14oz (400g) Gorgonzola Piccante
A small loaf of crusty bread
A jar of pitted black olives
1 ripe avocado
3 figs
2 peaches
A few handfuls each of strawberries and blueberries
A handful of almonds
A bunch of grapes
Runny honey, to serve
A handful of walnuts
Fresh basil leaves, to garnish

Take the cheeses out of the fridge 30 minutes before you want to serve them. Drain the mozzarella, tear it into shreds, and put it in a bowl. Slice the Gouda. You can leave the Gorgonzola whole or slice it. Arrange the cheeses on your grazing board. Slice a small loaf of bread, toast it, and arrange the toast on the board.

Drain the olives and add them to the board. Halve the avocado. Quarter the figs. Halve the peaches. Pop everything on the board, along with bowls of strawberries, blueberries, and almonds. Add a bunch of grapes, a dish of runny honey, a handful of walnuts, and garnish the board with basil leaves.

CONTINENTAL CHEESE & CHARCUTERIE GRAZING BOARD

PREP: 15 MINUTES • COOK: NIL • SERVES 4

This simple cheese and charcuterie board will take you on a tour of France, Spain, and Italy. The cheeses lean toward the rich and creamy—a classic French Brie, a triple cream Cambozola rippled with the same blue mold that's used to make Roquefort, and a mild goat cheese flavored with aromatic herbs. Salami and prosciutto are always crowd pleasers. Olives provide a savory hit of umami. Finally, there are guindillas. These are pickled green chili peppers from the Basque region of Spain, which are sweet and spicy and a great foil to the richness of the cheese and cured meats.

7oz (200g) petit Brie

4½oz (125g) goat cheese and herb roulade

6oz (170g) Cambozola Blue Brie

12 slices of salami di Milano

8 slices of prosciutto di Parma

A handful of salami sticks

A handful of mixed pitted olives

A handful of pickled guindillas

A few sprigs of rosemary, to garnish

Take the cheeses out of the fridge 30 minutes before you want to serve them.

Arrange the Brie, the roulade, and the Cambozola on your grazing board. Arrange the salami, prosciutto, and salami sticks on the board. Fill in the gaps with the olives and guindillas, garnish with a few sprigs of rosemary, and serve.

BRUNCH

CHEESY BREAKFAST TACOS

PREP: 10 MINUTES • COOK: 30 MINUTES • SERVES 4

A Tex-Mex favorite, breakfast tacos are a brilliant way to start the day. Often a mix of fluffy scrambled eggs, cheese, and grilled meats, I've added hash browns to these tacos to make them even more substantial. They're satisfyingly chunky and you can mix and match the extra toppings, depending on whether you'd like your taco to be richer (sour cream), tangier (lime juice), or spicier (pickled chilies). I've used a sharp Cheddar cheese in these tacos. If you prefer a lighter cheese, use crumbled Cotija or feta. If you'd like to add extra heat, a Pepper Jack studded with chilies, garlic, and rosemary is a mouthwatering choice.

14oz (400g) hash browns

8 rashers of streaky bacon

5oz (150g) mature Cheddar cheese

6 large eggs

2 tbsp butter

4 small flour tortillas

Sea salt, to taste

Pickled jalapeños, sliced scallions (spring onions), sour cream, and lime wedges, to serve

Cook the hash browns according to the packet instructions. Fry the bacon until crisp, then drain on paper towels (kitchen paper). Roughly chop it. Coarsely grate the cheese.

Crack the eggs into a bowl. Season with salt. Whisk well to combine. Add half the grated cheese to the eggs and stir to mix.

Melt the butter in a frying pan over a medium heat. Pour in the beaten eggs. Cook, stirring occasionally, for 3–5 minutes or until they're scrambled and set. Remove from the heat and set aside.

Warm the flour tortillas in a dry frying pan or microwave until soft and pliable.

Divide the cooked hash browns, scrambled eggs, cooked bacon, and remaining grated Cheddar cheese evenly among the tortillas.

Serve the breakfast tacos with pickled jalapeños, scallions (spring onions), sour cream, and lime wedges.

CHEESE & MUSHROOM OMELET

PREP: 5 MINUTES • COOK: 10 MINUTES • SERVES 1 • VEGETARIAN*

Fans of protein for breakfast will love this fast, feta-stuffed omelet. It takes just 15 minutes to make, and it's loaded not just with feta but also with tender caramelized mushrooms. Dry-frying the mushrooms in a pan without any seasoning helps ensure that they cook through and end up juicy without being wet and soggy. Feta is a creamy cheese with a salty, slightly sour flavor. It pairs really well with the earthy mix of eggs and mushrooms.

3oz (75g) mushrooms
1oz (25g) feta cheese
A handful of fresh flat
   leaf parsley leaves
3 medium eggs
1 tbsp olive oil
Sea salt and black
   pepper, to taste

* Feta can be vegetarian
   or not—always read
   the label

Brush clean and slice the mushrooms. Crumble the feta. Finely chop the parsley. Crack the eggs into a bowl and season with salt and pepper. Whisk together.

Set a frying pan over a medium heat. Add the sliced mushrooms and dry-fry, stirring occasionally, for 5–6 minutes or until browned and tender. Season with salt and pepper to taste. Scoop the mushrooms out of the pan.

Heat the olive oil in the empty frying pan. Pour in the beaten eggs, tilting the pan so they coat the base. Cook for 1–2 minutes or until the edges start to set.

Top half the omelet with the mushrooms. Sprinkle the crumbled feta over the top, then half the parsley. Use a spatula to fold the other half of the omelet over the mushrooms and feta. Cook for 1–2 minutes or until the eggs are set and the cheese has melted.

Slide the omelet onto a plate and garnish with the remaining chopped parsley. Serve straight away.

BACON, EGG & CHEESE MUFFIN

PREP: 5 MINUTES • COOK: 10 MINUTES • SERVES 1

There's a secret to getting a homemade bacon and egg breakfast muffin to taste like the muffins from your favorite fast food joint. It's an extra cooking step after you've fried the bacon and egg and toasted the muffin—you have to assemble the muffin, then wrap it up in foil and warm it through in the empty pan. The steam in the parcel softens the muffin and melts the cheese, giving this breakfast sandwich that familiar damp texture. The other secret is to use processed cheese slices—the plasticky, orange kind. They have the right flavor and they'll melt perfectly when you steam the muffin.

Rapeseed oil, for frying
2 bacon medallions
1 English muffin
1 medium egg
2 processed cheese slices
Ketchup or mayonnaise,
   to serve (optional)
Sausage patty or hash
   brown (optional)

Heat a frying pan over a medium heat. Grease it with a little oil and fry the bacon medallions for 3–4 minutes or until they're golden brown on both sides, flipping every so often. Remove the cooked bacon from the pan and drain on paper towels (kitchen paper).

While the bacon cooks, split the English muffin in half and toast it.

Grease an egg ring, place it in the frying pan and crack in the egg. Pop a plate over the top of the ring and fry the egg for 3–4 minutes or until the yolk is just set. Take the pan off the heat.

Place the bottom muffin half on a piece of foil. Top with the cheese slices, then the bacon. Lift the egg out of the pan and place it on top. Add a little ketchup or mayo, if liked. Cover with the other half of the muffin, then fold up the foil over it and seal to make a parcel.

Wipe the pan clean with paper towels, then pop it back over medium heat. Place the parcel in the pan. Warm the muffin through for 2 minutes. Remove from the heat, carefully unwrap the hot foil and serve.

To make this more substantial, broil (grill) a sausage patty and add to the muffin with the bacon, egg, and cheese. For a veggie version, swap the bacon for cooked hash browns.

COTTAGE CHEESE PANCAKES

PREP: 10 MINUTES • COOK: 30 MINUTES • SERVES 4 • VEGETARIAN

If you have a sweet tooth but still want your breakfast to pack some protein, these pancakes are for you. They're made with a tub of cottage cheese, which you quickly blitz into a batter in a blender. This recipe should make around 30 pancakes, but they're suitable for freezing, so you can cook a batch, then open-freeze them on a baking sheet before transferring them to a Ziplock bag. They'll keep in the freezer for around 3 months, and you can grill them from frozen. Serve the warm pancakes with fresh fruit, yogurt, and honey or syrup.

10oz (300g) cottage cheese
2 large eggs
1 tsp vanilla extract
4½oz (120g) all-purpose (plain) flour
1 tsp baking powder
2oz (50g) superfine (caster) sugar
Sea salt, to taste
Rapeseed oil or butter, for frying
Fresh fruit and honey, to serve

Tip the cottage cheese into a blender. Crack in the eggs and add the vanilla extract. Blend at high speed until smooth. Add the flour, baking powder, sugar, and a pinch of salt. Blitz again to combine.

Grease a frying pan with a little oil or butter and set over medium-high heat. Use a small ladle or scoop to pour in enough batter to make 3–4 pancakes. Keep them small—around 2½–2¾in (6–7cm) across is perfect. Fry for 1–2 minutes or until the top of the pancake is dry and the bubbles have burst. Flip the pancakes over and fry for another 1 minute. Transfer to a plate and keep warm in an oven set to its lowest temperature while you cook the rest of the pancakes. Regrease the pan as needed. You should be able to make approximately 30 pancakes.

Serve the pancakes warm with fresh fruit and honey.

CRISPY CHEDDAR WAFFLES

PREP: 20 MINUTES + RESTING • COOK: 40 MINUTES • MAKES 12 • VEGETARIAN

Swap your sweet waffles for savory ones and make these cheese-enriched, Belgium-style waffles this weekend. They make a brilliant base for a hearty brunch; you can load them up with eggs, bacon, and sausage, or use baked ham for a traditional farmhouse breakfast. Or keep things veggie by topping them with roast veg, refried beans, and a spoonful of guacamole or sour cream. Use a good, sharp Cheddar in the batter to pack in the flavor, and take the time to whisk up the egg whites and gently fold them into the batter—that's what gives these waffles their light and fluffy texture.

3½oz (100g) butter, plus extra for greasing
1lb 2oz (500g) all-purpose (plain) flour
4 tsp baking powder
19fl oz (550ml) buttermilk
4 medium eggs, separated
7oz (200g) mature Cheddar cheese
Sea salt, to taste

Melt the butter and set aside to cool. Sift the flour and baking powder into a large mixing bowl. Add a pinch of salt and whisk to mix the dry ingredients together.

Pour the buttermilk into a separate bowl and add the egg yolks (keeping the whites for later). Whisk to combine.

Add a splash of the buttermilk mixture to the dry ingredients and whisk in to make a thick paste. Slowly whisk in the remaining buttermilk mix until you have a smooth batter. Then whisk in the cooled melted butter. Cover the bowl with a clean tea towel and set aside for 30 minutes to rest.

Meanwhile, coarsely grate the Cheddar. Place the egg whites in a clean, grease-free, non-plastic bowl and whisk until they form soft peaks. Fold the egg whites into the batter with a metal spoon, trying not to knock out too much air. Fold in the Cheddar.

Set your oven to its lowest temperature and pop a heatproof plate in there. Grease your waffle irons and cook the batter following the manufacturer's instructions, transferring each waffle to the oven to keep warm while you cook the rest. This will take about 40 minutes in total. Serve straight away with your favorite toppings.

SUMMER FRUIT TOASTS

PREP: 10 MINUTES • COOK: 5 MINUTES • SERVES 4 • VEGETARIAN

Cottage cheese is everywhere at the moment; it's having a culinary renaissance, and you'll find it popping up in all sorts of dishes, from tender pancakes (see page 58) to creamy dips and sauces. But not everyone loves cottage cheese—it's the lumpy texture. If that's you, then you need to try this recipe for whipped cottage cheese. It's really easy, all you have to do is blend it in a food processor for a few minutes until it's smooth and velvety. You get all the light, refreshing flavor with none of the lumps. For these Summer Fruit Toasts I've added a drizzle of honey in with the cottage cheese. If you're making something savory, you can add in chopped herbs, pesto, or chili paste.

10oz (300g) cottage cheese
1 tbsp honey, plus extra for drizzling
14oz (400g) summer fruit, such as strawberries, raspberries, and blueberries
4 slices of bread
Fresh mint leaves, to garnish

Scoop the cottage cheese into a food processor, add 1 tablespoon honey, then run the processor for a couple of minutes until the cottage cheese is creamy and lump-free.

Prepare the fruit, if you need to. Toast the bread until golden brown and crisp.

Spread a generous amount of whipped cottage cheese on each slice of toasted bread. Top with the summer fruit, drizzle over a little honey, then garnish with the mint leaves. Serve straight away.

MINI CHEESE FRITTATAS

PREP: 20 MINUTES • COOK: 40 MINUTES • MAKES 6

These dainty egg muffins are a tasty way to use up leftover cooked veg. I've made them with roasted grape (cherry) tomatoes and kale, but you could swap in some leftover roast potatoes, sweet potato fries, cooked peas or broccoli, grilled Mediterranean veg, or, really, any veg you like. Just fold them into the beaten eggs with plenty of Parmesan and then bake until golden. They're delicious warm or cold, and they'll keep for up to 3 days in the refrigerator. They're a tasty grab-and-go choice.

Olive oil, for greasing
7oz (200g) grape (cherry) tomatoes
5oz (150g) kale
2oz (50g) Parmesan cheese
6 medium eggs
A handful of fresh basil leaves
Sea salt and black pepper, to taste

Preheat the oven to 350°F/180°C/Fan 160°C/Gas 4. Grease a 6-hole muffin pan (tin) with olive oil. Line a baking sheet with foil.

Halve the tomatoes, then tip them onto the baking sheet and season with salt and pepper. Roast for 20 minutes or until the tomatoes have softened and are a little charred.

Meanwhile, wash the kale, then strip the leaves off the woody cores and roughly chop them. Bring a small pan of water to the boil, add the kale and simmer for 2 minutes or until just wilted. Drain, rinse under cold water, then leave to drain.

Finely grate the Parmesan. Crack the eggs into a bowl, then add the Parmesan and season with salt and pepper. Whisk together until well combined. Tear in a few basil leaves and stir to mix.

Tip the kale onto paper towels and pat dry to get rid of any remaining water. Divide the kale and roasted tomatoes between the muffin pan holes. Pour the egg mixture over the veg, filling each hole almost to the top. Bake for 15–20 minutes, or until the frittatas are set and golden brown on top.

Let the mini frittatas cool in the tin for a few minutes before carefully removing them. Serve warm or at room temperature.

CHEESY HASH BROWN & BACON CASSEROLE

PREP: 15 MINUTES • COOK: 45–50 MINUTES • SERVES 6

This satisfying cooked breakfast is baked in a dish, so you can serve it by the slice. It's made with layers of all my breakfast favorites; the base is hash browns, topped with crisp bacon lardons and soft fried onions, and all covered with a mix of beaten eggs, Cheddar, and Emmental. Baked until golden, it's delicious served straight from the oven with hot sauce and toast. It's also good cold, especially as a filling for a chunky breakfast sandwich. Place a slice of the casserole in a soft roll with hot sauce and some sliced avocado. A fantastic portable breakfast that will keep you full until lunch.

Olive oil, for greasing and frying

7oz (200g) smoked bacon lardons

1 onion

6 large eggs

5oz (150g) mature Cheddar cheese

3½oz (100g) Emmental

5oz (150g) cottage cheese

14oz (400g) frozen hash browns, thawed

Sea salt and black pepper, to taste

Preheat the oven to 350°F/180°C/Fan 160°C/Gas 4. Grease a 5-pint (3-litre) baking dish with olive oil.

Set a frying pan over a medium heat. Add a little oil and the bacon lardons. Fry for 5 minutes, stirring often, until browned and crisp. Lift out of the pan with a slotted spoon and drain on paper towels (kitchen paper). Leave the oil in the pan.

While the bacon cooks, peel and finely chop the onion, then add to the pan and season with salt and pepper. Fry, stirring often, for 5–6 minutes or until the onion is soft and glossy. Take the pan off the heat.

Crack the eggs into a large mixing bowl, season with salt and pepper and whisk together. Coarsely grate the Cheddar and Emmental. Add half the grated cheese to the eggs with the cottage cheese and beat to combine.

Pat the thawed hash browns dry with paper towels, then arrange them in the greased baking dish. Top with the fried bacon and onions. Pour over the cheese and egg mixture. Scatter over the remaining grated cheese. Bake in the oven for 35–40 minutes, or until the casserole is set and golden brown on top.

Let the casserole cool for a few minutes before slicing and serving. This casserole can also be eaten cold and will keep for up to 2 days in the refrigerator.

HALLOUMI SHAKSHUKA

PREP: 15 MINUTES • COOK: 30 MINUTES • SERVES 2 • VEGETARIAN

Shakshuka means "all mixed up," and this version of the famous Middle Eastern dish is very mixed up. Instead of eggs poached in a spiced tomato sauce, it's made with slices of tender, fried halloumi. Originally from Cyprus, halloumi is a semi-soft cheese with a mild, salty flavor and a firm, rubbery texture. It can be eaten straight from the refrigerator, but it's brilliant used in cooking. The cheese softens without melting, which makes it ideal for bubbling in this dish's veggie-packed sauce. Frying it first gives it a golden crust, then cooking it in the sauce helps to soften it further. It still has that famous halloumi squeak when you bite into it, but with a velvety texture, too.

A pinch of saffron threads
1 onion
1 red bell pepper
1 yellow bell pepper
5oz (150g) grape (cherry) tomatoes
Olive oil, for frying
A handful of pitted black olives
1 tsp ground cumin
1 tsp ground coriander
14oz (400g) can of chopped tomatoes
7oz (200g) halloumi
A handful of fresh flat leaf parsley leaves
Sea salt and black pepper, to taste
Toasted pita breads, to serve

Grind the saffron threads to a powder using a pestle and mortar. Pop them in a bowl, add 2 tablespoons of water and set aside to soak.

Peel and finely chop the onion. Halve the peppers, scoop out the seeds and white pith, then finely slice them. Halve the tomatoes.

Set a large, deep-frying pan over medium heat and add a splash of olive oil. Add the onion, season with a pinch of salt and pepper, then fry, stirring occasionally, for 8–10 minutes or until the onion is glossy and hasn't picked up too much color.

Add the peppers, olives, and tomatoes to the pan, stir well, then pop a lid on the pan. Fry the veg for 5 minutes, stirring occasionally, until the peppers have softened.

Add the ground cumin and coriander to the veg. Cook and stir for 1 minute. Pour in the saffron water and the can of chopped tomatoes. Pour in 3½fl oz (100ml) water. Stir well, pop the lid back on the pan and bring it up to the boil. Turn the heat down and simmer for 8 minutes or until the sauce has thickened slightly.

Meanwhile, cut the halloumi block in half, then slice each half into 4 slices and pat dry with paper towels (kitchen paper). In a separate, dry pan, fry the halloumi over medium heat for 1–2 minutes on each side until golden brown.

Taste the sauce and add a pinch more salt and pepper, if needed. Add the halloumi to the sauce. Pop the lid back on the pan and gently simmer for 2–3 minutes or until the halloumi is soft. Meanwhile, roughly chop the parsley leaves.

Spoon the Halloumi Shakshuka into two warm bowls. Garnish with the chopped parsley and serve with toasted pita breads on the side.

CHEESE BLINTZES WITH CHERRY SAUCE

PREP: 15 MINUTES + RESTING • COOK: 30 MINUTES • MAKES 14–16 • VEGETARIAN

An Ashkenazi specialty, blintzes are thin pancakes stuffed with a sweetened curd cheese filling. These pancake parcels are then fried until they have crispy edges, which make a delicious contrast to the smooth, rich stuffing. You can eat them simply lightly dusted with sugar, but to make these pancakes really special, top them with a warm cherry compote. Enjoy as part of a weekend brunch.

FOR THE PANCAKES:

½oz (15g) butter
7oz (200g) all-purpose (plain) flour
1 tbsp superfine (caster) sugar
14fl oz (400ml) full-fat (whole) milk
2 large eggs
Clarified butter, for frying
Sea salt, to taste

FOR THE FILLING:

3½oz (100g) full-fat cream cheese
9oz (250g) semi-soft curd cheese
   or quark
2 tbsp superfine (caster) sugar
½ tsp vanilla extract

FOR THE CHERRY SAUCE:

15oz (425g) can of cherries
   in syrup
1 tsp cornstarch (cornflour)

Melt the butter in the microwave or in a small pan. Set aside to cool.

Sift the flour into a mixing bowl. Add a pinch of salt and the sugar and whisk together. In a separate bowl, whisk together the milk, eggs, and cooled melted butter. Pour it into the flour and whisk to combine. It should be a smooth batter that's as thick as heavy (double) cream. Cover the bowl with a clean tea towel and set aside to rest for 1–2 hours in the refrigerator.

Meanwhile, scoop the cream cheese into a mixing bowl and beat until it's smooth. Add the curd cheese, sugar, and vanilla extract. Beat to combine. Set aside in the refrigerator alongside the batter.

Tip the can of cherries and their syrup into a pan and stir in the cornstarch (cornflour). Gently warm over a medium heat for 4–5 minutes, stirring often, until the sauce has thickened. Set aside.

To make the pancakes, use clarified butter to lightly grease a 7in (18cm) heavy-based frying pan and place over a high heat. Add a ladleful of the batter and swirl it around to coat the bottom of the pan. Cook for 30 seconds–1 minute or until the bottom of the pancake is cooked. Flip and cook for a further 30 seconds. Slide out of the pan and repeat with the remaining batter. You should be able to make 14–16 pancakes in total.

Place 2 level tablespoons of the cream cheese mixture in the middle of each pancake and lift over the sides to cover the cheese. Lift the top and bottom end of the pancake over the middle to make a neat, rectangular parcel. You can make the blintzes a day ahead and store them in the refrigerator.

When you want to serve the blintzes, grease a large frying pan with clarified butter. Add the blintzes, in batches, seam-side-down. Fry for 1–2 minutes, then turn and fry for a further 1–2 minutes or until golden on both sides. Keep them warm in the oven, set to its lowest temperature. Reheat the cherry sauce. Serve the blintzes with the warm cherry sauce.

THE PERFECT GRILLED CHEESE

PREP: 5 MINUTES • COOK: 10–15 MINUTES • SERVES 1 • VEGETARIAN

I've tried lots of different hacks to make **The Perfect Grilled Cheese**, and I've concluded there are three crucial steps to get it just right. The first is using a mix of cheeses—something tangy and full of flavor, like Cheddar, as well as something that melts and is stretchy, like mozzarella. The second is spreading mayo on the outsides of the sandwich before frying to get that crisp texture. The final step is baking the sandwich in the oven for a few minutes. Lots of recipes promise the cheese will melt just by frying it in the pan, but I find nothing works better than a quick blast in a hot oven.

2oz (50g) mature
   Cheddar cheese
1oz (25g) mozzarella
1 tbsp butter
2 slices of white crusty
   bread
2 tbsp mayonnaise

Preheat the oven to 350°F/180°C/Fan 160°C/Gas 4. Coarsely grate the Cheddar. Drain the mozzarella and tear it into small pieces.

Melt the butter in a cast-iron frying pan over a medium heat. Add the bread slices and fry for 1 minute on one side, or until golden brown underneath. Lift out of the pan and pop them on your work surface, toasted side up. Take the pan off the heat.

Arrange the cheeses on one slice of the bread. Cover it with the other slice, making sure that toasted sides are on the inside. Spread 1 tablespoon mayonnaise over the top slice.

Wipe the frying pan clean and put it over a medium heat. Add the sandwich, mayo-side down. Fry for 2 minutes, pressing down with a spatula occasionally. It's ready to flip when it's golden brown underneath. Just before you flip it, spread the remaining mayonnaise on the top slice. Flip the sandwich and fry for another 1–2 minutes.

Transfer the pan to the oven. Bake for 5–8 minutes or until you can see the cheese has melted. Lift the sandwich out of the pan. Serve straight away by itself or with tomato soup or any preferred dip.

TOMATO SALAD WITH BURRATA

PREP: 10 MINUTES • COOK: NIL • SERVES 2 • VEGETARIAN

Burrata is mozzarella's glamorous cousin. It's a mozzarella case stuffed with stracciatella soft cheese and cream. While mozzarella is clean and light, burrata is oozing with indulgence. It's delicious popped on top of a tomato salad, as the sweetness and acidic tang of the tomatoes cuts through the cheese's richness. Add a simple balsamic dressing and fresh basil and you have the perfect summer lunch that's ready in less than 10 minutes.

14oz (400g) ripe tomatoes, room temperature

1 tbsp extra virgin olive oil

2 tbsp balsamic vinegar

4½oz (125g) burrata

A handful of fresh basil leaves

Sea salt and black pepper, to taste

Crusty bread, to serve

Cut the tomatoes into ¼in (½cm)-thick slices and arrange on a serving plate.

In a small bowl, whisk together the olive oil and balsamic vinegar with a pinch of salt and pepper. Drizzle the dressing over the tomatoes.

Place the ball of burrata on top of the tomatoes. Tear over a handful of basil leaves. Serve with crusty bread.

CHEESE & BLACK BEAN QUESADILLAS

PREP: 25 MINUTES • COOK: 45 MINUTES • SERVES 4 • VEGETARIAN

These cheese quesadillas make a brilliant prepare-ahead lunch. You can cook the beans and keep them in a tub in the refrigerator, ready to be used in quesadillas as you need them, or you can make and assemble the quesadillas, then open-freeze them on a baking sheet lined with parchment (baking) paper. Once they're frozen, transfer to freezeproof bags. They'll keep in the freezer for up to 2 months. Cook them from frozen in the microwave for a couple of minutes until warmed through, then crisp them up in a hot pan.

1 small red onion

Rapeseed or sunflower oil, for frying

1 fresh bay leaf

7oz (200g) tomatoes

1 garlic clove

1 tbsp pickled jalapeños

1 tsp ground cumin

½ tsp dried oregano

14oz (400g) can of black beans

3½fl oz (100ml) cold water

7oz (200g) Monterey Jack

8 small flour tortillas

Sea salt, to taste

Sour cream, guacamole, salsa, and salad, to serve

Peel and finely chop the onion. Warm a little oil in a pan over a medium heat and add the onion. Drop in the bay leaf. Season with a pinch of salt. Fry for 8–10 minutes, stirring occasionally, until the onion is soft and glossy.

Meanwhile, quarter the tomatoes and scoop out the seeds, then dice. Peel and crush the garlic. Drain the jalapeños and finely chop them.

Stir the tomatoes, garlic, and jalapeños into the onion. Add the cumin and oregano. Fry, stirring often, for 3–4 minutes or until the tomatoes have started to collapse.

Drain the beans and add them to the pan. Pour in the water. Stir well, pop a lid on the pan and cook the beans for 20 minutes or until warmed through and tender. Take off the heat and roughly crush the beans with a masher.

Coarsely grate the cheese. Place 4 small flour tortillas on

your work surface. Divide the mashed beans between them and top with the grated cheese. Cover with the remaining tortillas.

Heat a frying pan over a medium heat. Add one quesadilla to the pan and fry for 1–2 minutes or until golden brown underneath. Slide the quesadilla onto a plate, then flip it over back into the pan to cook the other side. Fry for another 1–2 minutes or until browned all over. Slide out of the pan and keep warm in an oven on its lowest setting while you cook the remaining quesadillas.

Slice the quesadillas into quarters. Serve with sour cream, guacamole, salsa, and salad.

WEDGE SALAD WITH BLUE CHEESE DRESSING

PREP: 10 MINUTES • COOK: 5–10 MINUTES • SERVES 2

A steakhouse favorite, wedge salad is a perfect mix of textures and flavors. The iceberg lettuce is crisp and refreshing while the blue cheese dressing is indulgently rich. The fried bacon adds crunch and there's a handful of tomatoes for sweetness. I've used Gorgonzola Dolce in the dressing to make a milder blue cheese sauce. But you could use Gorgonzola Piccante if you want your dressing to have a spicier blue cheese bite. Stilton and Danish Blue are also great choices for this salad.

4 rashers of streaky bacon
½ iceberg lettuce
7oz (200g) baby plum
   tomatoes
2 scallions (spring onions),
   green parts only
A handful of walnut
   halves

FOR THE BLUE CHEESE DRESSING:
3½oz (100g) Gorgonzola
   Dolce
3fl oz (75ml) sour cream
1 tbsp mayonnaise
1 tbsp lemon juice
1 garlic clove
Sea salt and black
   pepper, to taste

Start by making the dressing. Crumble the Gorgonzola into a mixing bowl. Add the sour cream, mayonnaise, and lemon juice. Peel and grate in the garlic. Beat together with a fork to make a dressing. Taste and add salt and pepper, if needed. Chill until ready to use.

Fry the bacon until crisp. Drain on paper towels (kitchen paper), then roughly chop it.

Cut the lettuce in half to make 2 chunky wedges, trimming off the root end. Halve the tomatoes. Finely chop the green parts of the scallions (spring onions). Roughly chop the walnuts.

Place each iceberg wedge on a serving plate. Add the tomatoes. Spoon the blue cheese dressing over the top. Sprinkle over the crispy bacon pieces, scallion greens, and walnuts. Serve straight away.

CROQUE MADAME

PREP: 10 MINUTES • COOK: 40 MINUTES • SERVES 1

When you want something extravagant for lunch, make a Croque Madame. A French café classic, it's an indulgent baked ham and cheese sandwich that's smothered in béchamel sauce and topped with a fried egg. The fried egg is what makes it a Croque Madame rather than a Croque Monsieur—the egg is supposed to look like a wide-brimmed lady's hat. The cheese of choice for this sandwich is Gruyère because it's earthy and nutty and melts well. You can swap it for Cheddar, Comté, Fontina, Emmental, or Gouda if you don't have Gruyère to hand.

1–2 tsp Dijon mustard

2 slices of French country bread

2 thick slices of ham

2oz (50g) Gruyère

1 tbsp butter

1 egg

FOR THE BÉCHAMEL SAUCE:

1 tbsp butter

1 tbsp all-purpose (plain) flour

4fl oz (125ml) full-fat (whole) milk

Sea salt, black pepper, and grated nutmeg, to taste

Preheat the oven to 400°F/200°C/Fan 180°C/Gas 6. Line a baking sheet with parchment (baking) paper.

Make the béchamel sauce. Melt the butter in a small pan over a medium heat. Add the flour and stir continuously with a wooden spoon for about 2 minutes to make a roux. Gradually add the milk while stirring constantly to avoid lumps. Gently simmer for 5 minutes or until the sauce thickens. Take off the heat, then season with salt, pepper, and freshly grated nutmeg. Set aside.

Spread a thin layer of Dijon mustard on two slices of bread. Place one slice of bread on the baking sheet, mustard-side-up, and top with the ham. Grate the Gruyère cheese and sprinkle three-quarters of it over the ham. Place the second slice of bread, mustard-side-down, on top to make a sandwich.

Pour the béchamel sauce evenly over the top of the sandwich. Top with the remaining Gruyère. Bake for 20–25 minutes or until the cheese is melted and golden brown.

When the sandwich is nearly baked, heat a small frying pan over a medium heat. Melt the butter in the pan, then crack in the egg. Fry for 2–4 minutes or until set to your liking.

Transfer the Croque Madame to a serving plate and top it with the fried egg. Serve straight away.

GREEK SALAD WITH MARINATED FETA

PREP: 30 MINUTES • COOK: NIL • SERVES 2 • VEGETARIAN*

In Greece this is known as *horiatiki*—village salad—and it's served in the summer when the veg are at their best. The combination of crisp cucumber, sharp red onions, juicy tomatoes, and salty feta is perfect hot-weather food. Normally the salad is topped with a slab of feta fresh from the barrel, but you can step up the flavors by marinating the cheese in a mixture of olive oil, lemon zest, and spices—I've used dried oregano and fennel seeds. If you want to spice things up, add a pinch of dried chili flakes, too.

7oz (200g) feta cheese
1 lemon
1 tsp dried oregano
½ tsp fennel seeds
2 tbsp extra virgin
   olive oil
1 red onion
9oz (250g) baby plum
   tomatoes
1 cucumber
1 Little Gem lettuce
3½oz (100g) pitted
   black olives
Sea salt and black
   pepper, to taste

* Feta can be vegetarian
   or not—always read
   the label

Drain the feta and pop it in a dish. Grate the lemon zest over the top (keep the lemon for later). Sprinkle over the dried oregano and fennel seeds. Drizzle over 2 tablespoons olive oil. Gently turn the feta to coat it in the oil and herbs (don't worry if it breaks up). Set aside to marinate for 15–20 minutes while you prepare the rest of the salad.

Peel and thinly slice the red onion. Halve the tomatoes. Slice the cucumber in half lengthwise, then roughly chop it. Slice the root off the lettuce, then roughly shred it.

Add all the veg to a salad bowl with the olives. Lift the feta out of the marinade and add to the veg.

Squeeze 1 tablespoon of juice from the lemon into the feta marinade. Season with salt and pepper and whisk to make a dressing. Taste and add more lemon juice, salt, or pepper, if needed. Drizzle over the salad and serve.

EASY VEGETABLE & RICOTTA TART

PREP: 25 MINUTES • COOK: 25–30 MINUTES • SERVES 4

This vegetable tart is a versatile standby when you want to make something that's easy and tasty but elegant-looking, too. It's made with a sheet of puff pastry, topped with a creamy layer of ricotta, Parmesan, and herbs. You can top it with your choice of vegetables; I've kept it simple with a layer of zucchini (courgettes). A layer of sliced tomatoes also works brilliantly. If you don't mind an extra step, you can top it with trimmed asparagus, purple sprouting broccoli, or string (green) beans that have been blanched in boiling water for 1–2 minutes. Roasted bell peppers or grilled eggplant (aubergine) slices are also a delicious choice.

1 zucchini (courgette), approximately 9oz (250g)

Olive oil, for drizzling

11oz (320g) ready-rolled puff pastry sheet

9oz (250g) ricotta

A large handful of fresh soft herb leaves, such as tarragon, dill, mint, or flat leaf parsley

1oz (25g) Parmesan cheese

1 lemon

2 garlic cloves

Milk, to glaze (optional)

Sea salt and black pepper, to taste

Preheat the oven to 400°F/200°C/Fan 180°C/Gas 6. Trim and thinly slice the zucchini (courgette) lengthwise and scoop the slices into a mixing bowl. Drizzle in a little olive oil. Season with salt and pepper, then gently turn the slices to coat them in the oil and seasonings. Set aside.

Unroll the sheet of puff pastry and place it on a baking sheet. Use a small, sharp knife to score a ¾in (2cm)-wide border around the edge of the pastry. Prick the centre of the pastry all over with a fork.

Tip the ricotta into a mixing bowl. Finely chop the herb leaves and add them to the ricotta. Finely grate in the Parmesan, then the lemon zest. Peel and grate in the garlic. Season with salt and pepper. Beat together.

Spoon the ricotta mixture into the middle of the tart and spread to cover it, leaving the border clear. Lay the zucchini slices over the top. Brush the pastry with a little milk, if you like, then bake for 25–30 minutes or until the pastry is golden brown and the zucchini slices are lightly charred. Serve warm or cold.

GRIDDLED HALLOUMI & HOUMOUS WRAPS

PREP: 5 MINUTES • COOK: 10 MINUTES • SERVES 2 • VEGETARIAN

Minimum cooking but maximum flavor is what I look for in a lunch. These wraps are layered with silky houmous, fresh salad, and fried halloumi. They take 15 minutes to put together and make a light, bright, nutritious meal. The combination of hot, fried halloumi and cool salad is delicious, but if you really want to cut down on the cooking time, you could swap the halloumi for crumbled feta or chunks of torn mozzarella.

¼ red bell pepper
6 grape (cherry) tomatoes
¼ cucumber
2 Greek-style flatbreads
3½oz (100g) halloumi
4 tbsp houmous/ hummus
A handful of mixed salad leaves

Scoop any white pith or seeds out of the red pepper chunk, then thinly slice it. Quarter the tomatoes. Dice the cucumber.

Place a frying pan over a medium heat. When it's warm, add the flatbreads and cook for 2–3 minutes, turning often, until soft, warm, and pliable. You may need to do this one at a time. Keep the warmed flatbreads wrapped in a clean tea towel while you cook the halloumi.

Slice the halloumi into thin fingers and add to the dry frying pan. Fry for 4–5 minutes, turning occasionally, or until the halloumi is golden brown. Take off the heat.

Spread the houmous over the flatbreads. Top with a handful of salad leaves, the red pepper, tomatoes, and cucumber. Lay the halloumi on top. Wrap the bread around the fillings and serve.

FRENCH ONION SOUP

PREP: 30 MINUTES • COOK: 1 HOUR 25–35 MINUTES • SERVES 4

If love could be dished up in a bowl, it would be French Onion Soup. This dish needs time, commitment, and passion. Just caramelizing the onions takes an hour, then you bubble them with wine and stock to make a richly flavored soup that's delicately fragranced with thyme and bay. Topping each bowl with toasted Gruyère croutons is the final indulgent touch.

1¾lb (800g) onions

3oz (75g) butter

3 tbsp olive oil

2 fresh bay leaves

4 fresh thyme sprigs, plus extra to garnish

4 garlic cloves

1 tbsp all-purpose (plain) flour

7fl oz (200ml) dry white wine

2½ pints (1½ litres) beef stock

8 slices of baguette

5oz (150g) Gruyère

Sea salt and black pepper, to taste

Peel and finely slice the onions. Melt the butter in a large pan over a low heat. Add the oil and the onions. Drop in the bay leaf and thyme sprigs, then season with salt and pepper. Pop a lid on the pan and very gently cook the onions for 20 minutes, stirring every 5–10 minutes, until soft.

Take the lid off the pan. Gently cook the onions for 40 minutes, stirring every 5–10 minutes, until the onions are well browned, sticky, and caramelized. If they start to dry out, add an extra chunk of butter and a ladleful of water.

Meanwhile, peel and grate or crush the garlic.

Lift the bay and thyme out of the onions. Turn the heat up to medium. Add the garlic and fry, stirring often, for 2 minutes or until aromatic. Stir in the flour, then pour in the wine, stirring, and bring it up to a bubble. Simmer for 2–3 minutes or until the wine has reduced by half.

Pour in the beef stock. Bring to a simmer, then turn the heat down and put the lid back on the pan. Simmer for 20–30 minutes or until the soup is rich and full of flavor. Taste and add salt and pepper, if needed.

While the soup simmers, preheat your grill. Place the baguette slices on a baking sheet and broil (grill) for 3–4 minutes, turning once, until lightly toasted. Coarsely grate the Gruyère and sprinkle it over the toasts, making sure they're well covered. Slide back under the grill for another 1–2 minutes or until the cheese has melted.

Ladle the soup into warm bowls. Top with the Gruyère toasts and garnish with a few thyme leaves. Serve straight away.

SPINACH, TOMATO & EMMENTAL QUICHE

PREP: 20 MINUTES + CHILLING • COOK: 1 HOUR 20–30 MINUTES • SERVES 8 • VEGETARIAN

This veggie quiche is made with Emmental. It's a mild, nutty-tasting cheese from Switzerland that's famously dotted with holes, which are created during the fermentation process. Carbon dioxide bubbles form while the cheese is being aged and become trapped in the cheese, creating the signature holes. Emmental is a great cooking cheese, often used in fondue (see page 40). It's perfect stirred into the filling for this quiche. Emmental's earthy sweetness pairs deliciously with spinach and tangy sun-dried tomatoes. Other Swiss cheeses will also work really well, depending on what you have available. Serve it warm or cold. It'll keep in the refrigerator for up to 3 days.

Flour, for dusting
14oz (400g) shortcrust pastry
Milk, to glaze
14oz (400g) spinach
3½oz (100g) Emmental
3½oz (100g) sun-dried tomatoes in oil
5 medium eggs
14fl oz (400ml) heavy (double) cream
¼ nutmeg
Sea salt and black pepper, to taste

Dust your work surface with flour. Roll out the pastry to make a 12in (30cm) circle. Roll the pastry around the rolling pin and then unroll it into a deep 11in (27cm) loose-bottomed tart tin. Trim the pastry and keep the trimmings in the refrigerator. Chill for 30 minutes.

Preheat the oven to 350°F/180°C/Fan 160°C/Gas 4. Prick the pastry case with a fork and line with parchment (baking) paper. Fill with baking beans and place the tart tin on a baking sheet. Bake for 30 minutes or until pale golden and almost cooked.

Remove the beans and paper, brush the pastry case with milk and bake for 15 minutes or until golden—you may need to cover the tart edges with foil to prevent them overbrowning.

Meanwhile, rinse the spinach, then tip it into a large pan. Wilt it over a medium heat, stirring often. Drain through a colander, then rinse with cold water to cool it. Shake off any excess water. Place the spinach in a tea towel and wring to squeeze out as much water as possible. Finely chop the spinach and set aside.

Coarsely grate the Emmental. Drain the sun-dried tomatoes. Arrange the spinach, Emmental, and sun-dried tomatoes in the pastry case.

Beat the eggs and cream together. Grate in the nutmeg and season with a little salt and black pepper, then pour the mixture into the tart case. Bake for 35–40 minutes or until just set.

Cool in the tin for 15–20 minutes, then lift the base out of the tin. Serve the quiche warm or cold with a optional side salad.

DINNER

PANEER TIKKA

PREP: 15 MINUTES + MARINATING • COOK: 10–15 MINUTES • SERVES 2 • VEGETARIAN

Paneer is a staple of Indian cooking. It holds its shape when it's heated so it's ideal for adding to vegetarian dishes, like this Paneer Tikka. The secret to packing flavor into these cheese skewers is to marinate the paneer in a mixture of yogurt and spices. The cheese soaks up the seasoning and you get a delicious contrast between the smooth, creamy paneer and the aromatic spices. Traditionally, Paneer Tikka is cooked in a tandoor oven, which gives it a touch of smoke, but grilling it at home in your oven is just as good. The skewers are also great cooked over a barbecue.

8oz (225g) paneer
1 red bell pepper
1 green bell pepper
1 red onion
Cilantro (coriander) chutney,
   salad, and roti, to serve

FOR THE MARINADE:
3½oz (100g) Greek yogurt
2 tbsp mustard oil
1 tbsp fresh lemon juice
½ tsp chili powder
1 tsp ground fenugreek
1 tsp turmeric
½ tsp garam masala
2 garlic cloves
1oz (30g) fresh ginger
Sea salt and black pepper,
   to taste

Start by making the marinade. Spoon the yogurt into a mixing bowl. Add the mustard oil, lemon juice, chili powder, fenugreek, turmeric, and garam masala. Peel and grate in the garlic and ginger. Add a pinch of salt and pepper and stir well to mix.

Chop the paneer into 12 cubes. Add to the marinade and gently turn to coat. Set aside to marinate for at least 30 minutes, or you can marinate it overnight in the fridge.

Halve the bell peppers and scoop out the white pith and seeds, then roughly chop. Peel the red onion and slice it into wedges.

Preheat your grill to high. Thread alternate chunks of paneer, red and green bell peppers, and red onion onto 4 skewers. Lay them on a baking sheet or on your grill rack and broil (grill) for 10–15 minutes, turning every few minutes, until lightly charred and the veg are just tender.

Serve the Paneer Tikka straight away with cilantro (coriander) chutney, salad, and warm roti.

FETA BAKED PASTA

PREP: 5 MINUTES + MARINATING • COOK: 40 MINUTES • SERVES 4 • VEGETARIAN*

This pasta dish was a viral sensation when it hit TikTok in 2020. To make it, all you do is roast a tray full of grape (cherry) tomatoes with a chunk of feta until they're lightly charred. Then mash them together, add in seasonings, and cook in the oven for a few more minutes to mingle the flavors. The oven does most of the work for you. There's almost no chopping and next to no washing up. Best of all, everyone always loves it.

1lb 5oz (600g) grape (cherry) tomatoes
7oz (200g) feta cheese
Olive oil, for cooking
2 garlic cloves
1 tsp dried oregano
½ tsp dried chili flakes
14oz (400g) pasta, such as casarecce, fusilli, or penne
A handful of fresh flat leaf parsley leaves
Sea salt and black pepper, to taste

* Feta can be vegetarian or not—always read the label

Preheat the oven to 400°F/200°C/Fan 180°C/Gas 6. Tip the tomatoes into a large ovenproof dish, then place the block of feta in the middle of the tomatoes. Drizzle over plenty of olive oil and season with salt and pepper. Bake for 30 minutes.

While the feta and tomatoes bake, bring a large pan of salted water to the boil. Peel and finely chop the garlic cloves.

After 30 minutes, take the dish out of the oven. Mash the feta and tomatoes together with a fork. Add the garlic, dried oregano, and chili flakes. Return to the oven and bake for 5–10 minutes or until the feta and tomatoes have browned a little.

Meanwhile, add the pasta to the boiling water and simmer for 8–10 minutes or until it's cooked but still with a little bite. Drain well.

Take the dish out of the oven. Tip in the drained pasta and toss to mix. Serve straight away, garnished with some fresh parsley and a drizzle of olive oil.

PUMPKIN & PARMESAN RISOTTO

PREP: 20 MINUTES • COOK: 45–55 MINUTES • SERVES 4

Risotto might be the original one-pan dish. At its simplest it's a silky combination of starchy, short-grain rice cooked slowly with stock and flavored with Parmesan. This version has golden saffron, thyme, and garlic bumping up the deliciousness, and the rice is cooked alongside nuggets of sweet pumpkin. You can use a wedge of the classic, orange-skinned pumpkin in this risotto, but it's good made with most varieties of squash. If you go pumpkin picking for Halloween, make sure you pick up a couple of edible gourds and turn them into this risotto.

A pinch of saffron threads

3½ pints (2 litres) chicken stock

1 onion

Olive oil, for frying

1¾lb (800g) wedge of pumpkin

2 garlic cloves

1lb 2oz (500g) arborio rice

A handful of fresh thyme sprigs

3½oz (100g) Parmesan cheese, plus extra to serve

Sea salt and black pepper, to taste

Crush the saffron to a powder using a pestle and mortar and scoop it into a pan. Pour in the chicken stock. Set it over a medium-low heat and gently bring to a simmer. When it has started to steam, take the pan off the heat.

Peel and finely chop the onion. Place a large pan over a low heat, drizzle in a little olive oil, then add the onion. Season with salt and pepper. Pop a lid on the pan and sweat the onion for 10 minutes, stirring occasionally, until the onion is soft.

Meanwhile, peel the pumpkin and remove any seeds and threads. Chop into chunks around ¼–½in (½–1cm) across. Peel and crush the garlic.

When the onion is soft, stir in the pumpkin and garlic. Cover with the lid again. Sweat for 10 minutes to soften the pumpkin.

Turn the heat up to medium, stir in the rice and cook, stirring, for 4–5 minutes or until the rice is a little translucent at the edges. Add a ladleful of the hot stock to the rice. Cook, stirring a few times, until the stock has been absorbed. Repeat until you have used up almost all the stock and the risotto is creamy and thick. You don't need to stir constantly, just every few minutes.

While the risotto cooks, pick the leaves off a few sprigs of thyme. Finely grate the Parmesan.

When you have just a few ladlefuls of stock left, add the thyme and the Parmesan. Cook and stir until the stock has been absorbed. This should take 20–30 minutes. Taste and add salt and pepper, if needed.

Ladle the risotto into warm bowls and serve with extra Parmesan and thyme.

FOUR CHEESE GNOCCHI

PREP: 10 MINUTES • COOK: 15 MINUTES • SERVES 4

This rib-sticking gnocchi dish is inspired by fonduta, Italy's answer to Swiss fondue. Fonduta is eaten in Piedmont, in Northern Italy, during the depths of winter, when a rich, hot cheese dip is a welcome way to ward off the cold. This sauce uses Fontina, the sweet, pungent cheese that is normally melted to make Fonduta. I've added buttery Taleggio, mellow blue Gorgonzola Dolce, and nutty Gruyère to the mix. It makes a luxurious sauce with a velvety texture that's perfect for coating potato gnocchi, or great stirred into pasta, too.

3½oz (100g) Gorgonzola Dolce
3½oz (100g) Taleggio
3½oz (100g) Fontina
2oz (50g) Gruyère
3½fl oz (300ml) heavy (double) cream
2¼lb (1kg) potato gnocchi
Sea salt and black pepper, to taste
Sage leaves, to garnish

Bring a large pan of salted water to the boil.

Crumble the Gorgonzola. Remove the rind from the Taleggio and chop it. Grate the Fontina and Gruyère.

Place a separate pan over a medium heat and pour in the cream. Warm, stirring, until starting to steam. Slowly add the cheese, a handful at a time, stirring well between each addition until it is all melted and smooth. Season with black pepper and take off the heat.

When the water in the other pan is boiling, add the gnocchi. Simmer for 4–5 minutes or until the gnocchi bob to the surface. Drain the gnocchi and add to the sauce (reheat the cheese sauce, if you need to). Gently stir to mix. Divide between warm plates and serve straight away.

CHICKEN PARMIGIANA

PREP: 25 MINUTES • COOK: 30–35 MINUTES • SERVES 2

Chicken Parmigiana is an Italian-American favorite. It's what you get when Northern Italian *cotoletta alla Milanese* and Southern Italian *melanzane alla parmigiana* meet on the East Coast of America. A crisp, breadcrumbed chicken breast is topped with red sauce—also known as marinara—and mozzarella, then baked until the cheese is melted and oozing. It's delicious served on top of a pile of spaghetti. Mozzarella might be the most obvious cheese in the dish, but there is Parmesan in the breadcrumb coating, and you can sprinkle a little extra over the top, just before serving.

2 boneless, skinless chicken breasts, approximately 1lb (450g)

2 tbsp all-purpose (plain) flour

1 medium egg

3oz (75g) breadcrumbs

1 tsp dried oregano

¾oz (20g) Parmesan cheese, plus extra to serve

Olive oil, for frying

14fl oz (400ml) marinara sauce

7oz (200g) mozzarella

5oz (150g) spaghetti

A handful of fresh parsley leaves

Sea salt and black pepper, to taste

Preheat the oven to 400°F/200°C/Fan 180°C/Gas 6. Line a baking sheet with parchment (baking) paper.

Place a chicken breast between two sheets of parchment paper. Use a meat mallet or rolling pin to bash it until it's ½in (1cm) thick. Set aside on a plate, then repeat with the second chicken breast.

Tip the flour onto a plate, season with salt and pepper and stir to mix. Crack the egg onto a second plate and beat well with a fork. Tip the breadcrumbs onto a third plate. Add the dried oregano and crack in some pepper. Finely grate the Parmesan and add to the breadcrumbs. Stir well to mix.

Dip a chicken breast in the flour, then shake off any excess. Dip it into the beaten egg, then dip it into the breadcrumbs, gently pressing them into the chicken to evenly coat. Set aside on a clean plate. Repeat with the second chicken breast.

Place a large frying pan over a medium-high heat. Drizzle in a little olive oil. Add the breadcrumbed chicken breasts and fry for 2–3 minutes on each side or until golden-brown. Transfer to the baking sheet.

Spoon two-thirds of the marinara sauce over the chicken. Drain the mozzarella and slice it. Place on top of the chicken. Bake for 25–30 minutes or until the cheese is melted, bubbly, and starting to brown.

While the chicken bakes, bring a large pan of salted water to the boil. When it's boiling, add the spaghetti and cook for 8–10 minutes, or until tender but with a little bite still. Drain the spaghetti, then return it to the pan. Pour in the remaining marinara sauce and gently warm over a low heat, stirring, until the sauce is warmed through.

Divide the spaghetti between two warm serving plates. Top with the chicken. Roughly chop some parsley and scatter it over to garnish. Serve with extra Parmesan.

STOVETOP MAC & CHEESE

PREP: 10 MINUTES • COOK: 35 MINUTES • SERVES 4

This ultra-creamy macaroni cheese is the ultimate one-pot pasta. It's a homemade version of the boxed mac and cheese that has been a kids' favorite since the 1930s. The pasta is cooked in the cheese sauce, so the pasta soaks up the flavor while also releasing its starch into the sauce, which helps give the dish its smooth consistency. A generous amount of Colby cheese provides a little orange color, while mozzarella adds a stretchy texture. If you can't get hold of Colby cheese, try using Red Leicester or Orange Cheddar. For a tangier flavor, swap the Colby for mature Cheddar or add in a handful of grated Parmesan.

5oz (150g) Colby cheese
4½oz (125g) mozzarella
2oz (60g) butter
2oz (60g) all-purpose (plain) flour
18fl oz (500ml) full-fat (whole) milk
1 tsp garlic granules
2 tsp Dijon mustard
Sea salt and white pepper, to taste
1¼ pints (700ml) hot chicken stock
10oz (300g) macaroni pasta
Sea salt and white pepper, to taste
Hot sauce, to serve
Cress, to garnish

Coarsely grate the Colby. Drain and coarsely grate the mozzarella. Set aside for later.

Melt the butter in a large pan set over a medium heat. Stir in the flour and cook, stirring, for 1–2 minutes to make a roux (a thick paste). Add a splash of milk and stir until the milk and roux are smoothly combined. Repeat, slowly adding the milk and stirring constantly, until you have a smooth white sauce.

Stir in the garlic granules and Dijon mustard. Season with a pinch of salt. Pour in the chicken stock and stir to mix. Tip in the pasta and stir well to mix. Bring the pan to a gentle simmer. When it starts to bubble, turn the heat down to low. Gently cook the pasta, stirring often, for 20 minutes or until the pasta is just tender but still with a little bite.

Add the grated cheeses to the pan and stir until melted and gooey. Taste and add salt or pepper, if needed. Serve the Mac & Cheese straight away, with hot sauce on the side.

TARTIFLETTE

PREP: 10 MINUTES • COOK: 35–45 MINUTES • SERVES 4

The main reason to go skiing in France isn't the snow or the stunning views, it's the food. Especially Tartiflette. This is a hearty dish of potatoes and bacon baked in cream with a round of pungent Reblochon De Savoie that's been fuelling French skiers for decades. Reblochon is an Alpine cheese that has a tender, washed rind and a luscious, creamy centre. It's mild and nutty tasting and perfect for baking. But it's not available everywhere, so this tartiflette is made with Camembert instead. Brie would also work well. Though if you can get hold of Reblochon, do use that to capture the flavor of the traditional French dish.

2 onions

2 tbsp butter

7oz (200g) unsmoked bacon lardons

2¾lb (1.25kg) waxy potatoes

2 garlic cloves

5fl oz (150ml) dry white wine

7oz (200g) Reblochon De Savoie, Camembert, or Brie

10fl oz (300ml) heavy (double) cream

Sea salt and black pepper, to taste

Peel and finely slice the onions. Set an oven-proof, cast-iron frying pan over a medium heat. When it's hot, add the butter, onions, and lardons. Turn the heat to low and fry, stirring often, for 10–15 minutes, or until the onions are soft and the lardons are well browned.

Meanwhile, preheat the oven to 400°F/200°C/Fan 180°C/ Gas 6. Bring a large pan of salted water to the boil. When it's boiling, add the whole, unpeeled potatoes and simmer for 10 minutes or until they're just starting to cook through. Drain and set aside to cool.

Peel and crush the garlic. Add it to the onions and lardons and fry, stirring, for 1–2 minutes, or until the pan is fragrant. Pour in the wine and simmer for 3–4 minutes or until the wine has mostly bubbled off. Take the pan off the heat and season with black pepper. Scoop the onions and lardons out of the pan.

When the potatoes are cool enough to handle, slice them into ¼in (½cm)-thick rounds. Cut the cheese in half through the middle so you have two round discs, then slice these in half to make four half-moons.

Arrange half the potatoes in the frying pan. Top with half the onions and lardons and half the cheese. Cover with the remaining potatoes. Then top with the remaining onions and lardons. Top with the remaining two cheese half-moons, making sure they're rind-side up. Pour over the cream. Bake for 20–25 minutes or until golden brown and bubbling. Serve straight away with an optional peppery green salad.

SIDES & SAUCES

MOZZARELLA STICKS

PREP: 30 MINUTES + FREEZING • COOK: 20 MINUTES • SERVES 4 • VEGETARIAN

There are a couple of tricks to making successful Mozzarella Sticks at home. The first is that you should use mozzarella cucina. It's a firm, dry version of mozzarella that was developed especially for cooking, as it melts perfectly. The second secret is to double coat the Mozzarella Sticks in egg and breadcrumbs. This should plug any gaps and prevent the cheese from leaking while it cooks. Finally, freezing the Mozzarella Sticks before cooking ensures that the breadcrumb coating has time to properly brown and crisp up before the cheese melts.

14oz (400g) mozzarella cucina
2 tbsp all-purpose (plain) flour
2 tsp dried oregano
2 medium eggs
5oz (150g) panko breadcrumbs
Sea salt and black pepper, to taste
Marinara sauce, to serve

Slice the mozzarella across the block to create squares approximately ½in (1cm) thick. Slice each square into 2 fingers.

Tip the flour onto a plate and add the dried oregano. Season with salt and pepper and stir to mix. Crack the eggs onto a separate plate and beat together. Tip the breadcrumbs onto a separate plate. Line a baking sheet with parchment (baking) paper.

Roll all the mozzarella fingers in the flour mix, then dip them in the beaten egg, then the breadcrumbs. Dip each finger in the egg and breadcrumbs again, making sure they are well coated. Arrange on the baking sheet and freeze overnight.

Line your air fryer baskets and heat the air fryer to 400°F/200°C. Arrange a single layer of the sticks in the baskets. Air-fry for 8–10 minutes or until golden brown. Transfer to a heatproof plate and keep warm in your oven, set to its lowest temperature. Repeat until you have cooked all the Mozzarella Sticks. Serve straight away with a dish of warm marinara sauce for dunking.

If you don't have an air fryer, you can bake the mozzarella sticks in the oven. Make and freeze them following the recipe. Preheat the oven to 400°F/200°C/Fan 180°C/Gas 6. Line a baking tray with foil and mist it with oil. Arrange the frozen Mozzarella Sticks on the tray and bake for 6–8 minutes, or until golden brown.

HALLOUMI FRIES

PREP: 20 MINUTES • COOK: 15–20 MINUTES • SERVES 4 • VEGETARIAN

Halloumi fries made their debut on a market stall in Camden in 2015 and quickly became a street food favorite. They're a Middle Eastern riff on Mozzarella Sticks (see page 112). Fingers of salty halloumi are dunked in a spiced batter and then fried or baked until crisp. Because halloumi has a high melting point, the fries are soft on the inside but they keep their shape. They're best eaten hot, so serve them as soon as they come out of the oven. A bowl of cool tzatziki on the side is the perfect dip to dunk them in.

14oz (400g) halloumi

3oz (75g) all-purpose (plain) flour

1 tsp ground cumin

1 tsp ground coriander

1 tsp smoked paprika

½ tsp turmeric

1 tbsp olive oil, plus extra for baking

3½fl oz (100ml) cold water

Sea salt and black pepper, to taste

Tzatziki, to serve

Preheat the oven to 400°F/200°C/Fan 180°C/Gas 6. Line a baking sheet with parchment (baking) paper.

Pat the halloumi dry with paper towels (kitchen paper) to remove any excess liquid. Cut the halloumi into 24 chunky fingers.

Tip the flour into a mixing bowl. Add the cumin, coriander, smoked paprika, and turmeric, then season with salt and pepper. Whisk together to mix. Pour in 1 tablespoon olive oil and half the water. Whisk to combine. Slowly trickle in the remaining water, whisking constantly, until you have a smooth, thick batter. You may not need all the water.

Dip each halloumi finger into the batter, ensuring they are evenly coated. Let any excess batter drip off, then transfer the coated halloumi to the baking sheet.

Bake the Halloumi Fries for 15–20 minutes or until golden brown and crisp. Serve straight away with a bowl of tzatziki for dipping.

CHEESE & POTATO GRATIN

PREP: 30 MINUTES + INFUSING • COOK: 1 HOUR 30 MINUTES • SERVES 6

Potatoes au gratin is a rich and luxurious side dish that goes brilliantly with grilled and roast meats or baked fish. It also makes a warming dinner on cold nights just by itself. This gratin is best made with waxy potatoes, like Pink Fir, Nicola, or fingerling potatoes. Waxy potatoes have less starch and a little bit more sugar than floury potatoes, and keep their shape when they're cooked, so they're perfect for thinly slicing and baking in a mixture of cream and Gruyère cheese.

18fl oz (500ml) heavy (double) cream

18fl oz (500ml) full-fat (whole) milk

2 garlic cloves

1 fresh bay leaf

2–3 fresh thyme sprigs

4½lb (2kg) waxy potatoes

2 onions

7oz (200g) Gruyère

Butter, for greasing

Sea salt and black pepper, to taste

Pour the cream and milk into a large pan. Peel and thinly slice the garlic and add to the pan. Drop in the bay leaf and thyme sprigs. Season with salt and pepper. Place the pan over a medium-low heat and bring to a simmer. Turn the heat down and gently bubble for 5 minutes, stirring occasionally. Make sure it doesn't boil. Take off the heat and set aside to infuse for 30 minutes.

Peel the potatoes and very thinly slice them—they should be ⅛in (¼cm) thick. Use a mandoline or the slicing attachment on a food processor, if you have one. Peel and thinly slice the onions. Coarsely grate the Gruyère. Preheat the oven to 350°F/180°C/Fan 160°C/Gas 4.

Lightly butter a 5-pint (3-litre) ovenproof dish. Arrange one-third of the potatoes and onions in the dish. Sprinkle over one-third of the Gruyère. Season with salt and pepper. Top with another third of the potatoes, onions, and cheese. Season again. Then top with the final layer of potatoes and onions and sprinkle over the remaining cheese.

Pick the bay and thyme out of the cream and pour it over the potatoes. Cover the dish with foil, crimping it tightly to the dish. Bake for 1 hour. Remove the dish from the oven and remove the foil, then return to the oven and bake for a further 15–20 minutes or until golden brown. The potatoes should be tender and a skewer inserted will go all the way through.

Let the gratin cool in the dish for a couple of minutes, then serve.

CHEESE GRITS

PREP: 5 MINUTES • COOK: 25–30 MINUTES • SERVES 4

An essential Southern side dish, Cheese Grits are good any time of day. Eat them topped with a fried egg or with cooked ham for breakfast. Serve them with buttery fried shrimp (prawns) or grilled fish for lunch. Or try them alongside pork chops for dinner. This recipe was made with regular grits, which are also known as quick grits and usually take around 20 minutes to cook. If you use old-fashioned, stone-ground grits, it will take a little longer and you may need extra chicken stock.

1½ pints (750ml) chicken stock
8fl oz (250ml) full-cream (whole) milk
7oz (200g) regular grits
5oz (150g) mature Cheddar cheese
2oz (50g) butter
4 tbsp heavy (double) cream
Sea salt and black pepper, to taste
Chopped chives, to garnish

Pour the chicken stock and milk into a medium-sized pan and bring to a gentle boil. Keep the heat set to medium-low. Gradually whisk in the grits, stirring constantly to prevent lumps from forming.

Reduce the heat to low and let the grits simmer, stirring occasionally, for about 20 minutes or until they're thick and creamy. If the grits become too thick, add more milk or chicken stock.

While the grits cook, coarsely grate the Cheddar.

Stir the butter into the cooked grits until the butter is melted and everything is combined. Gradually add the grated Cheddar, stirring continuously, until the cheese is fully melted and the mixture is smooth. Stir in the cream. Season with salt and pepper.

Spoon the grits into bowls and serve straight away.

ALIGOT

PREP: 15 MINUTES • COOK: 40–50 MINUTES • SERVES 4

A French specialty, Aligot is the silkiest, cheesiest way to make and serve mashed potatoes. It's traditionally made with Tomme Fraîche de l'Aubrac, which is a fresh, unsalted cheese with a supple texture and a delicate, floral flavor. It melts beautifully and gives Aligot its famous stretchiness. Tomme Fraîche can be hard to find outside of Southwest France, and although more aged French cheeses like Comté or Cantal will make a deliciously cheesy mash, they won't have quite the right texture. Instead, if you can't get hold of Tomme Fraîche, use a 75:25 mix of mild Cheddar and mozzarella.

1¾lb (800g) floury potatoes

10oz (300g) Tomme Fraîche de l'Aubrac

5oz (150g) butter

2 garlic cloves

7fl oz (200ml) heavy (double) cream

Sea salt, to taste

Put a large pan of salted water on to boil. Scrub the potatoes but leave the skins on. When the water is boiling, add the whole potatoes and simmer for 30–40 minutes, or until the potatoes are cooked through. A skewer should easily slide through a potato. Drain and set aside until they're cool enough to handle. Keep the pan for later.

Meanwhile, coarsely grate the cheese. Dice the butter. Peel and crush the garlic.

Peel the skins off the potatoes, then push them through a ricer into a large bowl, then use a masher to mash them even smoother.

Transfer the mash back to the pan over a low heat and add the garlic, butter, and cream. Cook, stirring with a wooden spoon, until it's smooth and creamy. Gradually add the grated cheese, beating well between each addition, until all the cheese is smoothly combined and the mash comes away from the side of the pan. It will be silky and shiny. Season with a little salt and serve.

NACHO CHEESE SAUCE

PREP: 5 MINUTES • COOK: 5 MINUTES • SERVES 4 • VEGETARIAN

Making your own Nacho Cheese Sauce is almost too easy. The secret is to use evaporated milk and a little cornstarch (cornflour)—it helps create that slightly thick, velvety texture that makes dipping nacho chips into the sauce so moreish. When it comes to the cheese, a smooth Monterey Jack is a good choice. It's buttery and creamy and adds a cheesy tang without too much funkiness. If you want to spice things up, use Pepper Jack. The chilies and bell peppers folded into the cheese will add an extra kick of heat to go with the pickled jalapeños. I've suggested adding a modest 1–2 teaspoons pickled jalapeños, but you can add more (or less) depending on how much heat you want your sauce to have.

5oz (150g) Monterey Jack
1–2 tsp pickled jalapeños
½ tbsp cornstarch
  (cornflour)
7fl oz (200ml)
  evaporated milk
Nacho chips, to serve

Coarsely grate the Monterey Jack. Drain the jalapeños and finely chop them.

Scoop the grated cheese, chopped jalapeños, and the cornstarch (cornflour) into a pan. Toss them together to coat the cheese.

Set the pan over a medium heat. Pour in the evaporated milk and gently heat, stirring constantly, for 4–5 minutes or until the cheese has melted and formed a smooth sauce. Serve straight away with nacho chips.

ALFREDO SAUCE

PREP: 2–3 MINUTES • COOK: 10 MINUTES • SERVES 4

Fettucine Alfredo is named after Alfredo di Lelio, a Roman restaurateur. He made his wife Ines a dish of fettucine, butter, and Parmesan to feed her up while she was convalescing after giving birth to their son. She loved it and told Alfredo to put it on his restaurant menu straight away. When the dish made its way over to America, cream was added and the sauce was served not just with pasta but with chicken, shrimp (prawns), and other seafoods. You can buy jars of Alfredo sauce, but it's so easy to make at home. In just 10 minutes, you'll have the richest, most indulgent cheese sauce ready to pour over cooked pasta.

3½oz (100g) Parmesan cheese
3½oz (100g) butter
9fl oz (250ml) heavy (double) cream
Sea salt and black pepper, to taste (optional)

Finely grate the Parmesan.

Place the butter in a deep frying pan, then pour in the cream and gently warm over a medium heat until melted. Stir to combine.

Add the Parmesan and stir to melt it into the sauce. Take off the heat and taste. Season with salt and pepper, if needed.

Serve with fettucine pasta, garnished with chopped parsley, or pour it over grilled chicken breasts, vegetables, or fish.

MORNAY SAUCE

PREP: 5 MINUTES • COOK: 10–15 MINUTES • SERVES 4

Mornay Sauce is one of the traditional sauces that form the basis of classic French cooking. Its mother sauce is béchamel, also known as white sauce. The difference between béchamel and mornay is cheese. Béchamel is a simple mix of flour, butter, milk, and nutmeg, but once you add cheese, it becomes mornay. You can stir cooked pasta into it to make a simple macaroni cheese or use it to make cauliflower cheese. It's also perfect for fish or chicken pies, and for spooning over cooked eggs, grilled chicken, or seafood.

3½oz (100g) Gruyère
2oz (50g) Parmesan cheese
2oz (50g) butter
2oz (50g) all-purpose (plain) flour
18fl oz (500ml) full-fat (whole) milk
1 medium egg yolk
Grated nutmeg and sea salt, to taste

Coarsely grate the Gruyère. Finely grate the Parmesan.

Melt the butter in a medium pan. Add the flour and whisk to make a smooth paste. This is your roux. Swap to a wooden spoon and cook, stirring constantly, for 2 minutes to cook off the flour.

Add a splash of the milk and beat it into the roux with the spoon. When it's smoothly combined, add another splash of milk and repeat. Continue until all the milk has been added. Add the egg yolk and beat to combine.

Stir in the grated cheeses. Season with a little nutmeg and salt, then taste and add more salt or nutmeg, if you think it needs it.

BLUE CHEESE SAUCE

PREP: 5 MINUTES • COOK: 10–15 MINUTES • SERVES 4

If you want to recreate a steakhouse vibe at home, then you have to make your own Blue Cheese Sauce. It's a bold and attention-grabbing sauce that elevates any dish it's served with. When it comes to which blue cheese to use in your sauce, use your favorite. I've used Stilton because I like its balance of sweetness and saltiness. Other blue cheeses, such as Roquefort, Maytag, Danish Blue, or Gorgonzola, will work just as well. Serve this sauce warm, spooned over steaks, burgers, or baked potatoes. Or pour it into a bowl and serve with breadsticks for dipping.

1 shallot
5oz (150g) Stilton
1 tbsp butter
9fl oz (250ml) heavy (double) cream
1 tsp Worcestershire sauce
½ tsp garlic powder
Sea salt and black pepper, to taste

Peel and finely chop the shallot. Crumble the Stilton.

In a small pan, melt the butter over a medium heat. Add the chopped shallot and cook, stirring, until softened and translucent, about 4–5 minutes.

Pour the cream into the pan. Bring to a gentle simmer over a medium-low heat, stirring occasionally.

Reduce the heat to low. Add the crumbled Stilton and stir until the cheese is melted and the sauce is smooth and creamy.

Stir in the Worcestershire sauce and garlic powder. Let the sauce simmer gently for another 2–3 minutes until slightly thickened.

Remove the sauce from heat. Season with salt and pepper and serve.

BAKING & DESSERTS

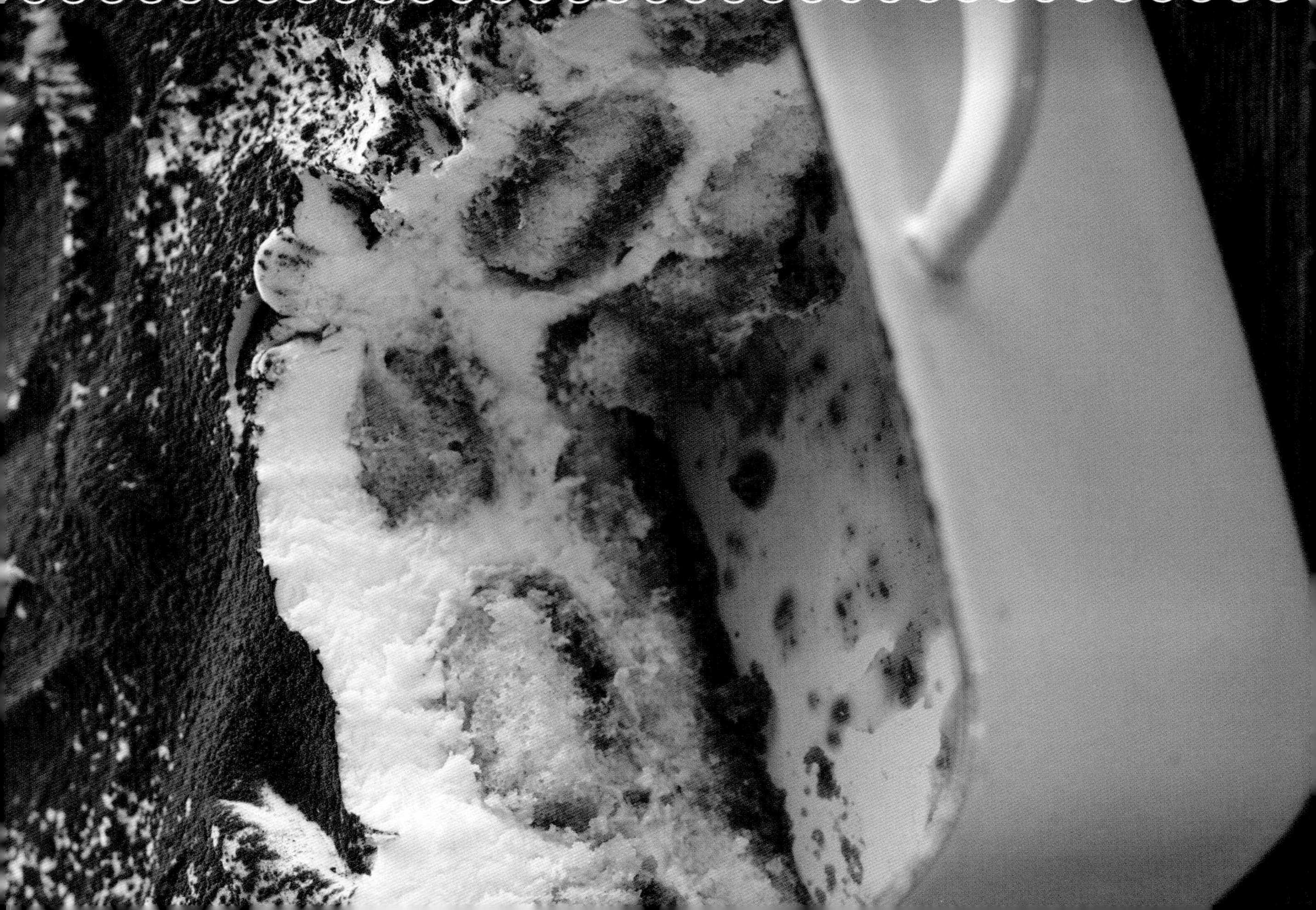

NEW YORK CHEESECAKE

PREP: 40 MINUTES + CHILLING • COOK: 1 HOUR–1 HOUR 30 MINUTES • SERVES 10 • VEGETARIAN

The classic rich and creamy New York Cheesecake is said to have been invented by Arnold Reuben at The Turf Restaurant. He's also supposed to have invented the Reuben sandwich, so we have a lot to thank him for. What made Reuben's cheesecake a revelation was the use of cream cheese instead of cottage cheese. It gave his cheesecake a firm, smooth texture and luxurious flavor. To ensure you get a velvety soft cheesecake, bake yours in a water bath, as it helps to cook the cheesecake all the way through, even at a low temperature. Let the cheesecake cool slowly after cooking, then chill overnight before serving. A good New York Cheesecake is so delicious it should be served plain, so you can appreciate the flavor of the cream cheese.

7oz (200g) butter, plus extra for greasing

14oz (400g) digestive biscuits

2lb (900g) full-fat (whole) cream cheese, room temperature

7oz (200g) superfine (caster) sugar

3 tbsp all-purpose (plain) flour

4 large eggs

1 tsp vanilla extract

9fl oz (250ml) sour cream

Zest of 1 lemon

Sea salt, to taste

Preheat the oven to 325°F/160°C/Fan 140°C/Gas 3. Grease a 9in (23cm) springform cake tin. Line the base and sides with parchment (baking) paper.

Melt the butter. Blitz the biscuits in a food processor until finely crushed. Pour in the melted butter and whizz a few more times to combine. Spoon the buttery crumbs into the tin and press them down firmly into the base. Refrigerate for 30 minutes.

Scoop the cream cheese into a large mixing bowl. Beat until smooth with an electric mixer. Beat in the sugar 1 tablespoon at a time, then beat in the flour. Crack in the eggs one at a time, beating well after each addition. Add the vanilla extract, sour cream, and lemon zest with a pinch of salt. Beat to combine.

Place the cake tin in the middle of a large sheet of foil.

Wrap the foil tightly around the sides of the tin. Pour the filling over the biscuit base. Place the cake tin in a roasting tin, then pour in enough boiling water to come halfway up the tin. Bake for 1 hour–1 hour 30 minutes or until the cheesecake is just set—the centre should have a slight shimmer when you gently shake the tin. Turn off the oven, open the door a little and leave the cheesecake to cool for 1 hour.

Lift the cake tin out of the roasting tin and set aside to cool completely. Once cooled, cover and refrigerate for 4 hours, or overnight, to set.

To serve, run a knife around the edge of the tin to loosen the cheesecake. Release the sides of the tin and transfer the cheesecake to a serving plate. Slice and serve.

BURNT BASQUE CHEESECAKE

PREP: 20 MINUTES • COOK: 30–40 MINUTES • SERVES 10 • VEGETARIAN

The dessert that conquered the internet, Burnt Basque Cheesecake is now firmly established as a contemporary classic. It was created in San Sebastián, in a tiny pintxo bar run by the Rivera family. In the 1980s, Santiago Rivera oversaw the kitchen and he experimented with recipes when the bar was closed. One of his ambitions was to create a cheesecake that would melt in the mouth. The Burnt Basque Cheesecake was the result. To get that essential light, silky texture when you're making it at home, take the cheesecake out of the oven while it's still molten in the middle and let it cool for a few hours at room temperature. You'll get a cheesecake that's delicate yet decadently rich.

1lb 9oz (700g) full-fat cream cheese, room temperature

7fl oz (200ml) heavy (double) cream

5oz (150ml) sour cream

9oz (250g) superfine (caster) sugar

4 large eggs

2 tbsp cornstarch (cornflour)

Zest of 1 orange

Sea salt, to taste

Preheat the oven to 450°F/230°C/Fan 210°C/Gas 8. Line the base and sides of a deep 9in (23cm) round cake tin with parchment (baking) paper, leaving some paper overhanging the sides to help lift the cheesecake out of the tin later.

Scoop the cream cheese into a mixing bowl. Beat with an electric mixer on its lowest setting until soft and smooth. Beat in the cream and sour cream. Add the sugar with a pinch of salt and slowly beat until the sugar has dissolved.

Beat in the eggs, one at a time. Scoop 4 tablespoons of the mix into another bowl, add the cornstarch (cornflour) to it and stir until smoothly combined. Return the cornstarch mix to the bowl. Add the orange zest and beat to combine.

Pour the cheesecake mixture into the tin. Bang the tin on the counter a few times to burst any bubbles. Bake for

30–40 minutes until the top is a deep, rich, dark brown, the sides are set, and the middle is still wobbly and liquid.

Remove from the oven and leave to cool for a few hours. Use the paper to lift the cheesecake out of the tin. Transfer to a serving plate and serve warm. Or, for neater slices, chill in the refrigerator for a few hours before slicing.

TIRAMISÙ

PREP: 30 MINUTES + 12–24 HOURS CHILLING • COOK: NIL • SERVES 8–10 • VEGETARIAN

In Italian, "tiramisù" means "pick-me-up," and it was given that name because the combination of coffee, eggs, and sugar is supposed to have an energizing effect on the diner. Personally, I find it so rich that I'm much more likely to need a short nap after eating it, but that never stops me ordering it. It's my favorite dessert. The layers of coffee-soaked sponge, whipped mascarpone, and cocoa powder are irresistible. A few shots of liqueur also add to the appeal. This is a dessert that you need to make ahead. Let it sit in the fridge for at least a day before serving it. This gives the layers time to soak and soften, giving the Tiramisù its moreish texture.

4 medium eggs

3oz (75g) superfine (caster) sugar

2lb (900g) mascarpone cheese

2fl oz (50ml) marsala wine

15fl oz (450ml) strong-brewed coffee, cooled

4fl oz (120ml) coffee liqueur

84 savoiardi sponge fingers

2oz (45g) cocoa powder

Crack the eggs and separate the yolks and whites into two clean, grease-free bowls. Use electric beaters to whisk the egg whites until stiff peaks form. Set aside.

Add the sugar to the egg yolks and beat with the electric beaters until pale, thick, and mousse-like. Beat in the mascarpone with a wooden spoon, then beat in the marsala. Fold the stiff egg whites into the mascarpone mix.

Combine the coffee and coffee liqueur in a bowl. Dip one-third of the savoiardi sponge fingers in the coffee and use them to line the base of a 7-pint (4-litre) dish. Top with one-third of the mascarpone mixture. Dust over enough cocoa powder to cover it.

Repeat with another one-third of the sponge fingers, dipping them in the coffee. Then top with another layer of mascarpone. Dust with cocoa powder to cover.

Repeat with the final sponge fingers, dipping them in the remaining coffee, and topping with the mascarpone mixture. Dust with a final layer of cocoa. Refrigerate for at least 12 hours. Tiramisù is best made 24 hours before you want to serve it.

The dish contains raw eggs, so it may not be suitable for young children, the elderly, and people with compromized immune systems.

RICOTTA DONUTS

PREP: 10 MINUTES + CHILLING • COOK: 30 MINUTES • MAKES 30 • VEGETARIAN

These fluffy little donuts aren't quite instant, but they are faster than making traditional yeasted donuts. The batter takes a few minutes to whisk up and is enriched by a tub of ricotta. When you're frying the donuts, keep them small and don't overheat the oil. It's a good idea to fry one donut to start with to check the timings; when it looks cooked, slice it open to see if it is cooked all the way through. This will tell you if you need to lower the temperature or make your donuts smaller. They should be tender and light with a crisp crust.

9oz (250g) ricotta

3oz (75g) superfine (caster) sugar, plus extra for dusting

2 oranges

2 large eggs

5oz (150g) all-purpose (plain) flour

2oz (50g) cornstarch (cornflour)

2 tsp baking powder

Sunflower or rapeseed oil, for deep-fat frying

Drain the ricotta, then tip it into a mixing bowl. Add the sugar. Finely grate in the zest of both oranges. Squeeze in the juice from half an orange. Crack in the eggs and whisk together until smooth.

Sift in the flour, cornstarch (cornflour), and baking powder and fold to combine. You should have a thick, sticky batter. Refrigerate for 1 hour.

Pour enough oil into a large pan to fill it one-third of the way up, or use a deep-fat fryer. Heat to 325°F/170°C. A cube of bread dropped into the oil should brown within 30 seconds.

When the oil is hot, scoop up teaspoons of batter from the mix and carefully drop them into the oil. Keep them relatively small so they cook through. You should be able to fit 4–6 donuts in your fryer, depending on the size.

Fry for 6–7 minutes, turning the donuts frequently so they brown all over. They should be a rich brown colour. Lift out of the hot oil and transfer to a plate lined with paper towels (kitchen paper) to drain. Repeat with the remaining batter. You should be able to make around 30 small donuts.

Shake 3–4 tablespoons sugar onto a plate and roll the donuts in it to lightly coat. Serve straight away. These donuts are best eaten warm.

CHEESE BÖREK

PREP: 30 MINUTES • COOK: 25–30 MINUTES • SERVES 4–6 • VEGETARIAN*

A favorite dish in the Ottoman Court—although it was made and enjoyed for centuries before that—Börek is an elegant treat. It's made with layers of flaky filo pastry that can be filled with sweet or savory fillings. This Cheese Börek is stuffed with a mix of salty feta and cottage cheese, along with a pinch of fresh parsley. Börek can be eaten any time of day; with tea or coffee for breakfast, with salad for lunch, or as part of a meze spread for dinner. It can be a casual street food snack, or part of a formal dinner. There's no occasion that can't be improved by a slice of Börek.

3½oz (100g) butter
7oz (200g) feta cheese
5oz (150g) cottage cheese
A handful of fresh flat leaf parsley leaves
4½oz (125g) filo pastry sheets
Milk, to glaze (optional)
Black pepper, to taste

* Feta can be vegetarian or not—always read the label

Melt the butter and set aside.

Crumble the feta into a mixing bowl. Add the cottage cheese and beat together to combine. Finely chop the parsley and add it to the cheese. Crack in a little pepper and stir to combine. Set aside.

Preheat the oven to 350°F/180°C/Fan 160°C/Gas 4. Take a sheet of filo pastry and lay it on your work surface—leave plenty of space to the right (or left, if you prefer). You're going to make a long "snake" of pastry. Brush the filo all over with melted butter. Take the next sheet of filo and lay it to the right of the pastry, overlapping by about 6in (15cm). Brush with butter. Repeat with the remaining pastry and butter, overlapping the sheets to create a chain of pastry sheets. If you have butter left over, set it aside for later.

Spoon the cheese filling along the bottom edge of the pastry to make a long snake. Carefully roll the pastry up around the filling until you have a long pastry snake filled with cheese. Take one end of the snake and gently fold it in, turning the pastry snake round and round until you have a spiral.

Transfer it to a baking tray. Brush the remaining butter over the Börek. If you don't have any butter left, glaze it with a little milk. Bake for 25–30 minutes or until golden brown.

Carefully slide the cooked Börek onto a serving plate. Serve warm from the oven in slices. The Börek can be kept in the refrigerator for up to 3 days and eaten cold.

CHEESE SCONES

PREP: 20 MINUTES • COOK: 10 MINUTES • MAKES 12 • VEGETARIAN

These scones are one of the quickest and most delicious cheese treats you can bake. With featherlight middles and a crunchy, golden-brown crust, they are incredible served warm straight from the oven. Split them open and top with a pat of salted butter. They make a fantastic breakfast or teatime snack. I've used a mature Cheddar in them to make sure they have a good, strong cheesy flavor, but you can use any sharp, well-flavored hard cheese. If you only have a milder cheese on hand, like Colby, swap 1–2oz (25–50g) of it for Parmesan to bump up the richness.

1lb 5oz (600g) self-rising (self-raising) flour, plus extra for dusting
1 tsp baking soda (bicarbonate of soda)
1 tsp baking powder
9oz (250g) mature Cheddar cheese
2 medium eggs
10fl oz (300ml) buttermilk
Milk, to glaze
Sea salt, to taste

Preheat the oven to 400°F/200°C/Fan 180°C/Gas 6. Dust a baking tray with a little flour.

Sift the flour, baking soda (bicarbonate of soda), and baking powder into a large mixing bowl. Add a pinch of salt. Whisk together to mix. Coarsely grate the cheese and add it to the bowl, keeping back about 2oz (50g) for sprinkling. Stir to mix.

Beat the eggs and buttermilk together. Pour the buttermilk mix into the flour. Stir the dry and liquid ingredients together with your hand to bring it together and make a soft, dryish dough.

Dust your work surface with a little flour and turn out the dough. Knead briefly to bring together. Pat it into a round approximately 1in (2½cm) high. Stamp out 12 rounds using a 2¾in (7cm) fluted cutter.

Place the scones on the baking tray. Brush the tops with milk. Top with the remaining cheese.

Bake for 10 minutes or until the scones lift easily off the baking tray and feel light. Cool on a wire rack for 15 minutes before serving. Serve warm with butter.

INDEX